Patterns in the Sky

The Nature of Science S2

Weather Patterns D4

Motions in the Sky D32

HOUGHTON MIFFLIN

BOSTON

Printed in the U.S.A.   ISBN-13: 978-0-547-06238-9   ISBN-10: 0-547-06238-9   2 3 4 5 6 7 8 9-DOW-16 15 14 13 12 11 10 09

Do What Scientists Do

Meet Fernando Caldeiro, the astronaut. His friends call him Frank. He is training to go into space. When he is not training, he tests computer programs used to run the space shuttle. Before Mr. Caldeiro became an astronaut, he tested new jets. He also worked on space shuttle rockets.

Frank Caldeiro is floating in a jet that gives the feeling of low gravity. This jet is one tool scientists use to learn more about space.
The jet's nickname is the "vomit comet." Can you guess why?

Many Kinds of Investigations

Astronauts carry out many investigations in space. Sometimes they observe Earth and take photos. Other times they do experiments. They may test how plants or animals react to low gravity. They share what they find out with other scientists.

Astronauts learn to fly the space shuttle in machines called simulators. They also learn to use space shuttle tools to collect information.

Think Like a Scientist

Everyone can do science. To think like a scientist you have to:

- ▶ ask a lot of questions.

- ▶ find answers by investigating.

- ▶ work on a team.

- ▶ compare your ideas to those of others.

What is this lizard doing? Is it sleeping? Is it waiting for insects to fly by? Or, is it doing something else?

Use Critical Thinking

When you know the difference between what you observe and what you think about your observation, you are a critical thinker. A fact is an observation that can be checked to make sure it is true. An opinion is what you think about the facts. When you ask someone, "How do you know that?" you are asking for facts.

The lizard lies under the heat lamp for a while. Then it gets food. **I wonder if it must warm up before it can move around?**

I read that a lizard's body temperature falls when the air cools. It warms itself by lying in the sun.

Science Inquiry

You can use **scientific inquiry** to find answers to your questions about the world around you. Say you have seen crickets in the yard.

Observe It seems like crickets chirp very fast on some nights, but slowly on other nights.

Ask a question I wonder, does the speed of cricket chirping change with temperature?

Form an idea I think crickets chirp faster when it's warmer.

Experiment I will need a timer and a thermometer. I will count how many times a cricket chirps in 2 minutes. I will do this when the air temperature is warmer and when the air temperature is cooler.

Conclusion I counted more chirps in warmer air temperatures. This result supports my idea. Crickets chirp faster when it is warmer.

Scientific inquiry includes communicating what you learn. You can tell about your experiment in words or drawings. Tell others to try it themselves. You can expect them to get the same results.

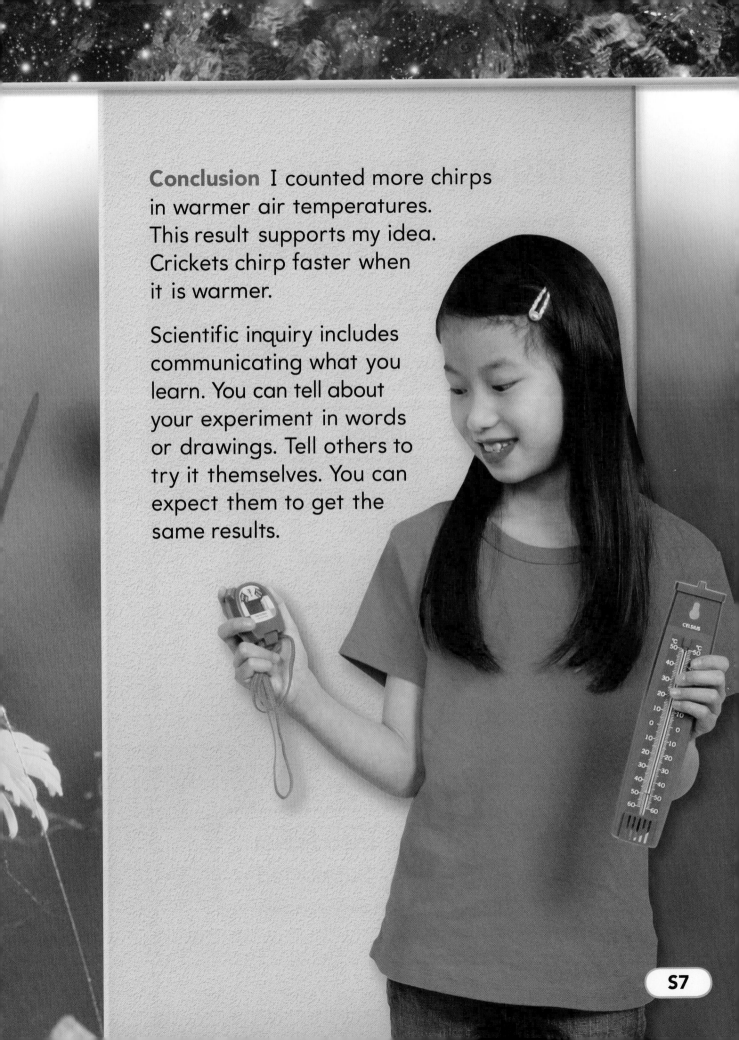

Inquiry Process

Here is a process that some scientists follow to answer questions and make new discoveries.

```
        Observe
           ↓
     Ask a Question
           ↓
      Form an Idea
           ↓
    Do an Experiment
           ↓
    Draw a Conclusion
         ↙        ↘
  Idea Is      Idea Is Not
 Supported      Supported
```

Try it Yourself!

Experiment With Bouncing Balls

Both balls look the same. However, one ball bounces and the other one does not.

1. What questions do you have about the balls?

2. How would you find out the answers?

3. Write an experiment plan. Tell what you think you will find out.

Be an Inventor

Lloyd French has enjoyed building things and taking them apart since sixth grade.

Mr. French invents robots. They are used as tools to make observations in places where people cannot easily go. One of his robots can travel to the bottom of the ocean. Another robot, called Cryobot, melts through thick layers of ice—either in Antarctica or on Mars. Cryobot takes photos as it moves through the ice.

"If you want to be a scientist or engineer, it helps to have a sense of curiosity and discovery."

S10

What Is Technology?

The tools people make and use are all **technology.** A pencil is technology. A cryobot is technology. So is a robot that moves like a human.

Scientists use technology. For example, a microscope makes it possible to see things that cannot be seen with just the eyes. Measurement tools are used to make their observations more exact.

Many technologies make the world a better place to live. But sometimes solving one problem causes others. For example, airplanes make travel faster, but they are noisy and pollute the air.

A Better Idea

"I wish I had a better way to _____".
How would you fill in the blank?
Everyone wishes they could do something
more easily. Inventors try to make those
wishes come true. Inventing or improving
an invention takes time and patience.

Kids have been riding
on scooters for many
years. These newer
scooters are faster.
The tires won't get
flat. They are also
easier to carry from
place to place.

How to Be an Inventor

① **Find a problem.** It may be at school, at home, or in your community.

② **Think of a way to solve the problem.** List different ways to solve the problem. Decide which one will work best.

③ **Make a sample and try your invention.** Your idea may need many materials or none at all. Each time you try it, record how it works.

④ **Improve your invention.** Use what you learned to make your design better.

⑤ **Share your invention.** Draw or write about your invention. Tell how it makes an activity easier or more fun. If it did not work well, tell why.

Make Decisions

Plastic Litter and Ocean Animals

It is a windy day at the beach. A plastic bag blows out of sight. It may float in the ocean for years.

Plastic litter can harm ocean animals. Sometimes sea turtles mistake floating plastic bags for jellyfish, their favorite food. The plastic blocks the stomach, and food cannot get in. Pelicans and dolphins get tangled up in fishing line, six-pack rings, and packaging materials. Sometimes they get so tangled that they cannot move.

Deciding What to Do

How can ocean animals be protected from plastic litter?

Here's how to make your decision. You can use the same steps to help solve problems in your home, in your school, and in your community.

Learn → Learn about the problem. You could talk to an expert, read a science book, or explore a web site.

List → Make a list of actions you could take. Add actions other people could take.

Decide → Decide which action is best for you or your community.

Share → Explain your decision to others.

Science Safety

Know the safety rules of your classroom and follow them. Read and follow the safety tips in your science book.

- ▶ Wear safety goggles when your teacher tells you.

- ▶ Keep your work area clean. Tell your teacher about spills right away.

- ▶ Learn how to care for the plants and animals in your classroom.

- ▶ Wash your hands when you are done.

EARTH SCIENCE

UNIT
D

Patterns
in the Sky

EARTH · UNIT D · SCIENCE

Patterns
in the Sky

Reading in Science................. D2

Chapter 8
Weather Patterns.................. D4

Chapter 9
Motions in the Sky D32

═ Independent Reading ═

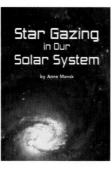

My First Snow

Star Gazing in our Solar System

Maria Mitchell

Discover!

Why doesn't it snow everywhere in winter?

Think about this question as you read. You will have the answer by the end of the unit.

D1

THE SUN

OUR NEAREST STAR

by Franklyn M. Branley
illustrated by Edward Miller

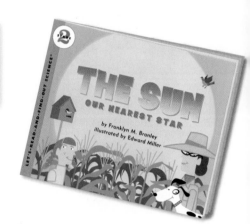

D2 • Unit D

The sun is very big. It is much bigger than Earth. The sun is almost a million miles across. If Earth was the size of a pea, the sun would be the size of a beach ball.

Chapter 8

Weather Patterns

water cycle

evaporates

water vapor

condenses

precipitation

season

hibernate

migrate

condenses

Water vapor condenses, or changes to drops of water.

precipitation

Water that falls from clouds is called precipitation.

hibernate

Some animals hibernate, or go into a deep sleep.

migrate

Some animals migrate, or move to warmer places in fall.

How Does Weather Change?

Science and You

When the weather changes, you may need to change your plans for the day.

Inquiry Skill

Use Numbers You can use numbers to compare temperatures.

What You Need

thermometer

Daily and Weekly Weather					
	Monday	Tuesday	Wednesday	Thursday	Friday
Morning					
	Temperature____°F	Temperature____°F	Temperature____°F	Temperature____°F	Temperature____°F
Midday					
	Temperature____°F	Temperature____°F	Temperature____°F	Temperature____°F	Temperature____°F
Afternoon					
	Temperature____°F	Temperature____°F	Temperature____°F	Temperature____°F	Temperature____°F

weather chart

Compare Weather

Steps

1. **Observe** See whether it is sunny, cloudy, raining, or snowing. Record what you see.

2. **Measure** Find the outdoor temperature. Record your findings.

3. **Use Numbers** Repeat steps 1 and 2 two more times during the day. Compare the temperatures you recorded.

4. Repeat steps 1–3 for a week.

Think and Share

1. What changes did you observe during any one day?

2. **Infer** What can you infer about morning temperatures?

STEP 1

STEP 2

STEP 3

Investigate More!

Experiment Make a plan to measure rainfall. Talk with others about your findings.

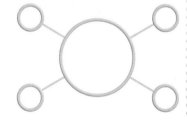

Learn by Reading

▶ Vocabulary

water cycle

evaporates

water vapor

condenses

precipitation

▶ Reading Skill

Main Idea and Details

Daily Weather Patterns

Weather changes in patterns over time. Weather can change from day to day. Weather can also change throughout a day.

The air is often warmer in the afternoon than it is in the morning. The Sun warms the air during the day. Then the air gets cooler again at night. These changes in temperature are measured with a thermometer.

a storm over Tampa, Florida

Sudden Changes

Sometimes weather can change very quickly. It might be a calm and clear day. Then a storm appears, bringing rain, thunder, and lightning in the afternoon.

Scientists called meteorologists use tools to study the weather. They tell what kind of weather is coming. They use radar to keep track of weather changes.

▶ **MAIN IDEA** How might weather change during a day?

The radar shows rain around the Tampa area.

light rain   rain   heavy rain

Tampa

The Water Cycle

Heat from the Sun warms land, water, and air. The Sun's heat causes water to change form and move. Water moving from Earth to the air and back again is called the **water cycle**.

▶ **MAIN IDEA** How does the Sun change water?

2 Water as a gas is called water vapor. You cannot see it. It mixes into the air.

1 The Sun warms the water. The water evaporates, or changes to a gas.

3 Air with water vapor rises into cooler air. Water vapor condenses, or changes to drops of water. These drops of water form clouds.

4 As the drops get bigger, they get heavier. The drops fall to the ground as rain, snow, sleet, or hail.

5 Rain and melted snow collect in streams, rivers, lakes, and oceans. The water cycle begins again.

Precipitation and Wind

Water that falls from clouds is called **precipitation**. Rain, snow, sleet, and hail are kinds of precipitation. When the air is warm, rain falls. When the air is cold enough, snow may fall. If falling snow melts and refreezes, it changes to sleet. When falling rain is tossed about in cold air, it freezes into balls of ice. These balls of ice are called hail. Hail often forms during thunderstorms.

◄ hail

Storms bring wind with rain. ▼

snowstorm
with drifts

Wind is moving air. Wind can be gentle, or it can be very strong. During many storms, a strong wind blows. Strong wind can blow falling rain or snow. Wind can blow fallen snow into drifts.

▶ **MAIN IDEA** **What are two different kinds of precipitation?**

Lesson Wrap-Up

❶ **Vocabulary** What happens to water when the Sun heats it?

❷ **Reading Skill** What happens to water in the water cycle?

❸ **Use Numbers** A morning temperature is 50°F. What might an afternoon temperature be?

Technology Visit **www.eduplace.com/scp/** to find out more about weather.

What Is the Pattern of the Seasons?

Science and You

Knowing the pattern of the seasons helps you know the best time to plant seeds.

Inquiry Skill

Communicate You can communicate by talking to others about what you find out.

What You Need

goggles

water and soil

2 thermometers

Measure Heat

Steps

1. Put the cups of soil and water in a refrigerator overnight.

STEP 1

2. **Measure** Remove the cups from the refrigerator. Measure and record the temperature of each material.

STEP 2

3. **Record Data** Put the cups in a warm, sunny place for 20 minutes. Record the temperature of each material again.

Think and Share

1. **Communicate** Tell how the temperature of each material changed.

STEP 3

2. **Infer** The thermometers measured the amount of heat absorbed. What was the source of heat?

Investigate More!

Ask Questions Think about other times when the temperatures of materials might change. What questions would you ask?

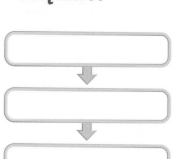

Weather Patterns of the Seasons

A **season** is a time of year. Winter, spring, summer, and fall are the four seasons. They occur in this order every year. <u>Each season has its own weather pattern.</u>

Air temperatures change with the seasons. Winter is the coolest. Summer is the warmest. In spring temperatures slowly rise. In fall temperatures slowly fall.

Compare the thermometers. How is the winter temperature different in these places?

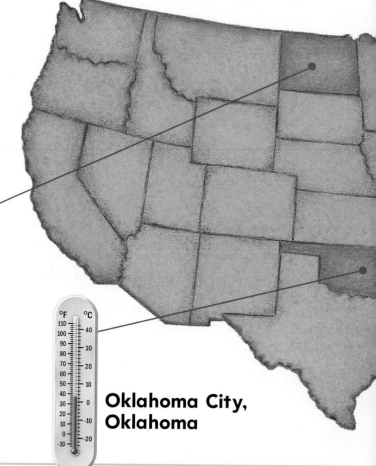

Bismarck, North Dakota

Oklahoma City, Oklahoma

Weather patterns are different from place to place. In some places, winter weather is very cold. In other places, winters are just a little cooler than summers. Some places have about the same amount of precipitation in all four seasons. In other places, one season is very wet and the others are dry.

▶ **SEQUENCE** How do temperatures change as the seasons change?

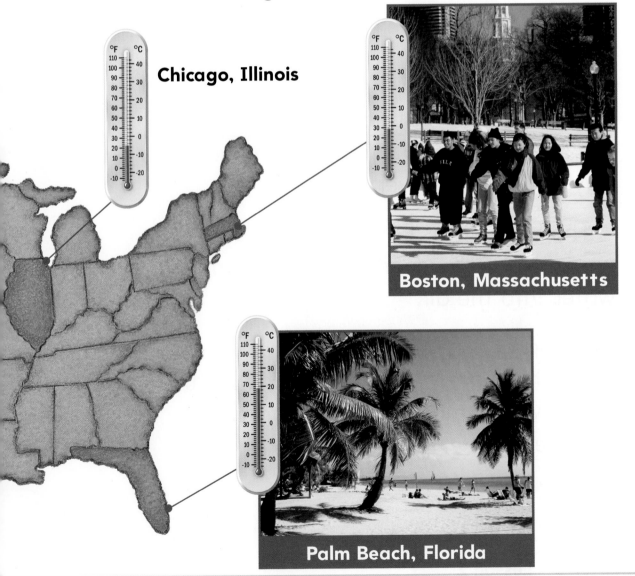

Chicago, Illinois

Boston, Massachusetts

Palm Beach, Florida

winter

Winter days have the fewest hours of daylight.

spring

In spring, daytime slowly gets longer.

Daylight Patterns

The Sun shines in the daytime. The number of daylight hours changes with the seasons. This pattern of changing daylight repeats every year.

The Sun warms Earth's land and water. Heat moves from the land and water into the air.

The land, air, and water get warmer when there are more hours of daylight. This is why summer has the warmest weather.

summer

Summer days have the most hours of daylight.

fall

In fall, the daytime slowly gets shorter.

▶ **SEQUENCE** How does the number of daylight hours change as the seasons change?

Lesson Wrap-Up

❶ **Vocabulary** What is a **season**?

❷ **Reading Skill** Which season comes after the one with the most daylight hours?

❸ **Communicate** Tell why summer has the warmest weather.

🖥 **Technology** Visit **www.eduplace.com/scp/** to find out more about seasons.

Focus On

Health and Safety

STAYING SAFE IN THE SUN

Too much sunlight is not healthful. It can harm your skin and damage your eyes.

You need to protect your skin and eyes from the Sun's rays in all seasons. The Sun's rays are strongest midday. If you must be outdoors at that time, try to stay in the shade. Cover your skin with tightly woven, lightweight clothing.

The Sun's rays can be harmful even when it is cold outdoors. The Sun's light can reflect off snow.

How is this child keeping safe in the Sun?

Safety in the Sun

Wear sunscreen to protect your skin. Put it on before you go outdoors.	
Wear a hat with a brim to protect your neck, ears, and face.	
Wear sunglasses to protect your eyes.	
You sweat more in warmer weather. Drink a lot of water to replace the water you lose.	

Sharing Ideas

1. **Write About It** Make a list of things you do outdoors in warm weather. Write about how you can stay safe.

2. **Talk About It** Talk with your classmates about Sun safety at school. Make a class list of ways to keep safe while outdoors.

How Do Living Things Change With the Seasons?

Science and You

Knowing how living things change with the seasons helps you know when you might see baby animals.

Inquiry Skill

Compare Tell how objects are alike or different.

What You Need

2 cups and 2 bags

2 thermometers

ice cubes

different fabrics

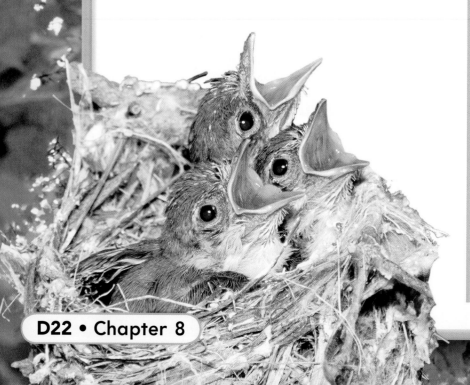

Compare Fabrics

Steps

1. Put an ice cube in each bag. Wrap a piece of fabric around each bag.

STEP 1

2. Place a fabric-wrapped bag in each cup. Slide a thermometer into each cup as shown.

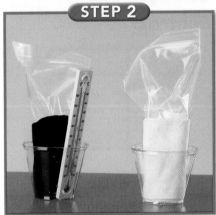
STEP 2

3. **Compare** Wait 15 minutes. Compare the temperatures on the thermometers. Record what you observe.

STEP 3

Think and Share

1. Heat moved from the air through the fabric and into the ice. Which fabric kept the air warmer?

2. **Infer** Which fabric would be good to wear in cold weather? Tell why.

Investigate More!

Be an Inventor Make a container to keep ice from melting. Tell about the materials you would use.

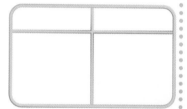

▶ **Reading Skill**
Compare and
Contrast

Plants and the Seasons

Changes in the seasons cause plants to change. Plants change as the air slowly warms or cools. They change as the number of daylight hours changes.

Changes with the Seasons

Season	spring
How a Sweet Gum Tree Changes	Leaves grow and flowers bloom.

In spring, many plants flower. In summer, the fruits grow. Some plants have leaves that change color in fall. Where winters are very cold, plants stop growing.

▶ **COMPARE AND CONTRAST** How are plants different in spring and summer?

summer	fall	winter
piny fruits form. eeds form inside he fruits.	Leaves turn red and fall. Seeds spread.	Leaves and most of the fruits have fallen. The seeds rest.

Animals and the Seasons

Animals change with the seasons. Some change how they look. Most change what they do. The fur of some animals gets thicker in the fall and stays thick all winter. The fur may change color, too.

In fall, the antlers are fully grown. The deer's fur gets thicker.

In spring, a male deer's antlers begin to grow.

It is hard for animals to find food in winter. Some animals collect food in fall to store for winter. Other animals **hibernate**, or go into a deep sleep. In spring they come out of hibernation. They find food and have their young.

▲ Ground squirrels hibernate in winter.

Some animals **migrate**, or move to warmer places in fall. The animals can find food in these warm places.

▲ A ground squirrel comes out of its burrow in spring.

▶ **COMPARE AND CONTRAST** How are a deer's antlers different in spring and fall?

Some monarch butterflies migrate in fall.

Dressing for the Seasons

<u>People change the things they do with the seasons.</u> As the weather changes, people wear different clothes.

A hat helps keep in body heat.

Layers of clothes keep heat near your body.

Socks and sturdy shoes keep your feet warm and dry.

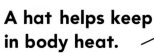

Lesson Wrap-Up

❶ **Vocabulary** What do animals do when they **hibernate**?

❷ **Reading Skill** Tell how a plant is different in two seasons.

❸ **Compare** Tell how an animal is different in two seasons.

📱 **Technology** Visit **www.eduplace.com/scp/** to find out more about living things in seasons.

LINKS
for Home and School

Math **Read a Chart**

The chart shows weather data for the summer months in Akron, Ohio.

Weather in Akron, Ohio	June	July	August
Rain	3 inches	4 inches	3 inches
Temperature	68°F	72°F	71°F
Clear Days	7	7	8
Cloudy Days	12	11	11

1. Tell about the weather in July.

2. Which month had the most clear days?

Social Studies **Winter Activities**

Kayla lives in Florida. Jason lives in Michigan. They drew pictures of themselves having fun in winter. Tell how winter is different in these two places. Write about winter where you live. Draw a picture of yourself having fun in winter.

Visual Summary

Weather, plants, and animals change with the seasons.

Patterns of Change

Season	Winter	Spring	Summer	Fall
Temperature	coolest	slowly rises	warmest	slowly falls
Plants				
Animals				

Main Ideas

1. Is air temperature usually warmer in the morning or afternoon? Tell why. (p. D8)

2. Why does water evaporate? (p. D10)

3. List the seasons in the order in which they occur. (p. D16)

4. What do animals do in fall to get ready for winter? (pp. D26–D27)

Vocabulary

Choose the correct word from the box.

5. A time of year

6. When water vapor changes to drops of water

7. Water that falls from clouds

8. Water moving from Earth to the air and back again

> **water cycle**
> (p. D10)
>
> **condenses**
> (p. D11)
>
> **precipitation**
> (p. D12)
>
> **season** (p. D16)

Test Practice

Choose a word to complete the sentence.

9. Water as a gas is _____.

   migrate   water vapor   water cycle   season

Using Science Skills

10. **Compare** Draw the same tree or plant in winter and spring. How are the drawings alike and different?

11. **Critical Thinking** Why would a place have fewer hours of daylight in fall than in summer?

Motions in the Sky

Sun

solar system

planet

rotates

revolve

orbit

Moon

phases

star

constellation

solar system

The Sun and the space objects that move around it make up our solar system.

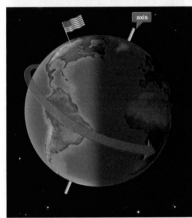

rotates

Earth rotates, or spins around an imaginary line.

phases

The different ways the Moon looks are called phases.

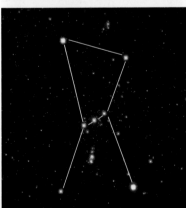

constellation

A constellation is a group of stars that forms a picture.

What Makes Up the Solar System?

Science and You

Knowing about the solar system helps you see how important the Sun is to the planets.

Inquiry Skill

Predict Use what you observe and know to tell what you think will happen.

2 thermometers

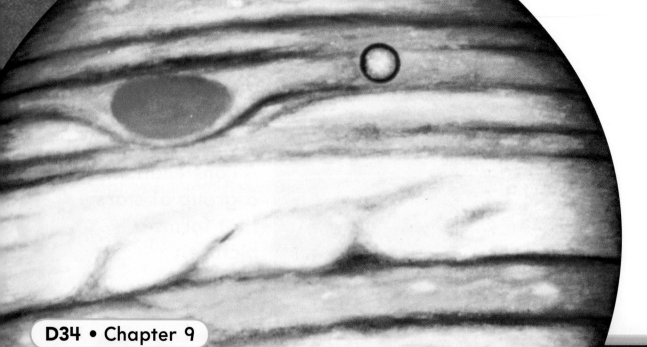

Light and Heat

Steps

STEP 1

1. Put one thermometer in a sunny place. Put the other thermometer in a shaded place.

2. **Predict** Record the temperature shown on each thermometer. Predict how the temperatures will change.

3. **Record Data** Wait 15 minutes. Record the temperatures again.

STEP 2

	First Time	Second Time
Sun	_____ °F	_____ °F
Shade	_____ °F	_____ °F

Think and Share

1. How did what you observed compare to what you predicted?

2. **Infer** How did the temperatures change? Tell why.

STEP 3

Investigate More!

Experiment Do the activity a few more times. Compare your findings. Were they the same each time? Tell why or why not.

▶ **Vocabulary**

Sun

solar system

planet

▶ **Reading Skill**
**Main Idea
and Details**

The Sun

The **Sun** is the brightest object in the day sky. The Sun is much larger than Earth. It looks small because it is very far away. The Sun is made of hot gases that give off energy. The Sun's energy reaches Earth as light. Some of this light is changed to heat.

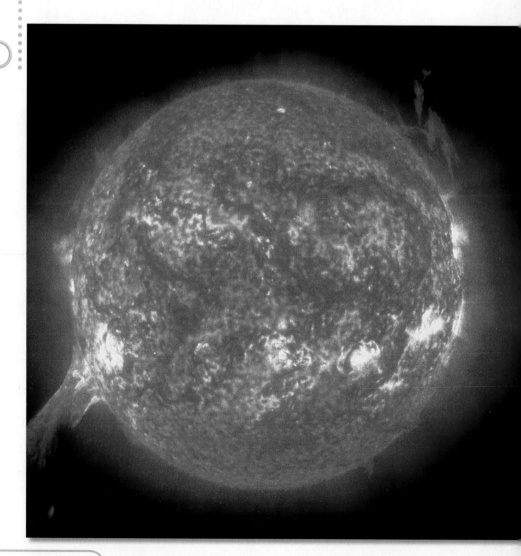

Living things on Earth use energy from the Sun. Land, air, and water are warmed by the Sun. The Sun keeps people and animals warm. Light from the Sun helps people and animals see. It helps plants live and grow.

▶ **MAIN IDEA** How do living things use energy from the Sun?

Plants use the Sun's light to make their own food.

The rocks are warmed by the Sun's heat.

The Solar System

The Sun and the space objects that move around it make up our **solar system**. There are eight planets in our solar system. A **planet** is a large object that moves around the Sun. Planets are always in the sky. Many planets have moons. Earth is a planet with one moon.

▶ **MAIN IDEA** What makes up the solar system?

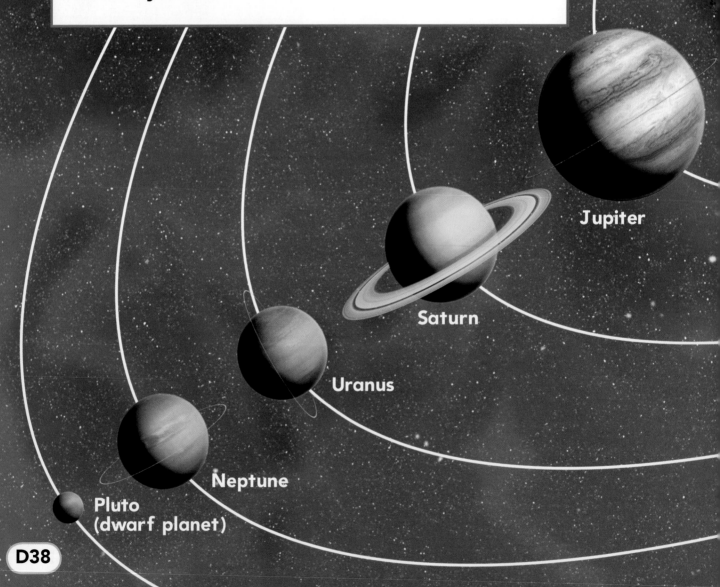

Jupiter

Saturn

Uranus

Neptune

Pluto
(dwarf planet)

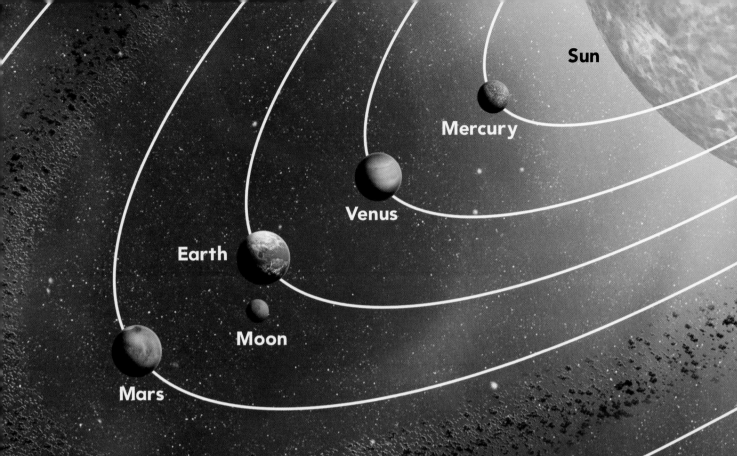

Sun

Mercury

Venus

Earth

Moon

Mars

Lesson Wrap-Up

❶ **Vocabulary** What is a **planet**?

❷ **Reading Skill** How do living things use the Sun's energy?

❸ **Predict** What might happen to a plant if it did not get enough light from the Sun? Tell why.

Technology Visit **www.eduplace.com/scp/** to find out more about the Sun.

How Does Earth Move?

Science and You

Knowing how Earth moves helps you understand day and night.

Inquiry Skill

Observe Use your senses to find out about something.

What You Need

large sheet of paper

marker

ruler

Observe Shadows

Steps

STEP 1

1. Go outdoors. Place a large sheet of paper on the ground. Make an X in the center of it.

2. **Observe** Hold the ruler as shown. Trace its shadow. Write the time.

STEP 2

3. Put an arrow on your drawing to show where the Sun is in the sky. **Safety:** Do not look right at the Sun!

4. Repeat steps 2 and 3 two more times during the day.

STEP 3

Think and Share

1. How did the length and position of the shadow change during the day?

2. **Infer** What caused the shadow to change?

Investigate More!

Work Together Work with a partner. Use a flashlight and different objects to make shadows. Discuss what materials make shadows. Tell how the shadows change.

▶ **Vocabulary**

rotates

revolve

orbit

▶ **Reading Skill**

Draw Conclusions

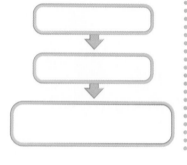

Earth Spins

Each day the Sun seems to move across the sky. But the Sun does not move. Earth **rotates**, or spins around an imaginary line. The line is called an axis. It takes Earth 24 hours, or one day, to rotate one time.

As Earth rotates, different parts face the Sun. When the part where you live faces the Sun, you have day. When the part where you live faces away from the Sun, you have night.

Where is it day in this picture?

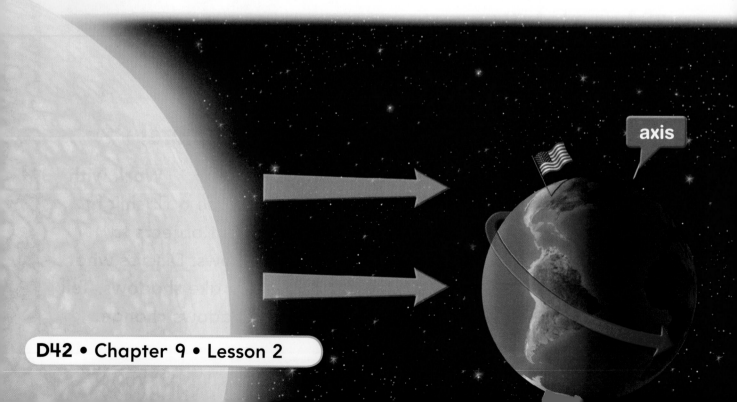

axis

Shadows Change

Light from the Sun shines on Earth. Shadows form when an object blocks sunlight. As Earth rotates, shadows change length and position. People can tell time by observing the Sun and shadows.

morning In the morning, the Sun is low in the sky. Shadows are long. They grow shorter and shorter until noon.	
noon At about noon, the Sun is at its highest point in the sky. Shadows are shortest.	
afternoon In the afternoon, the Sun is low in the sky again. Shadows grow longer.	

▶ **DRAW CONCLUSIONS** At what time during the day is your shadow its shortest?

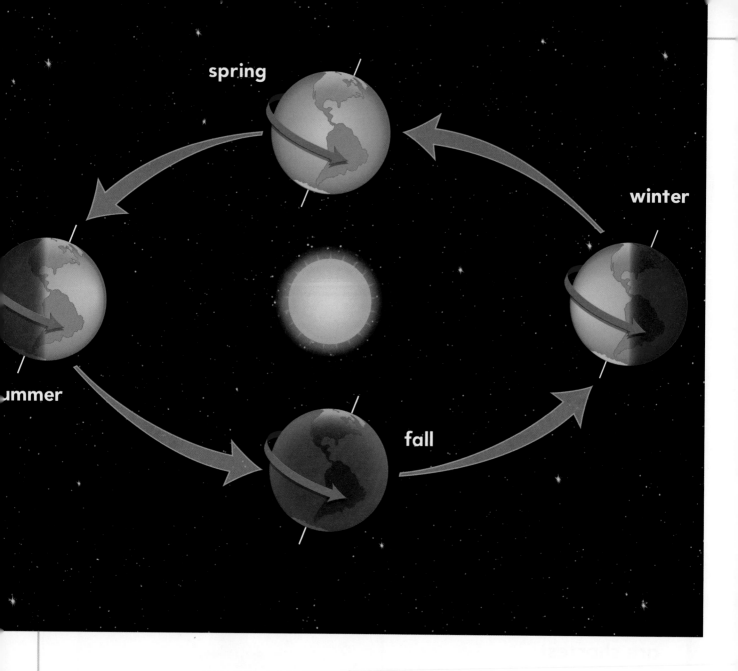

Earth Moves Around the Sun

While Earth rotates, it also moves in another way. Earth and the other planets **revolve**, or move in a path, around the Sun. The path that one space object travels around another is called an **orbit**. It takes one year for Earth to revolve around the Sun.

During Earth's orbit, the seasons change. When our part of Earth is tilted toward the Sun, we get more direct light from the Sun. It is summer. As Earth revolves around the Sun, our part of Earth tilts away from the Sun. Sunlight hits our part of Earth on a slant, so we get less light. Then it is winter.

▶ **DRAW CONCLUSIONS If it is spring, how long will it be until it is spring again?**

Lesson Wrap-Up

❶ **Vocabulary** Which of Earth's movements takes one year?

❷ **Reading Skill** When the United States has night, where is it day?

❸ **Observe** What happens to shadows throughout the day?

🖥 **Technology** Visit **www.eduplace.com/scp/** to find out more about Earth's movements.

How Does the Moon Move?

Science and You

Knowing how the Moon moves helps you understand why it looks different each night.

Inquiry Skill

Use Models Use a model to learn about the Moon.

What You Need

lamp

Moon model

Moon chart

Moon Phases

Steps

STEP 1

1. **Use Models** Place a lamp on a table in a darkened room. The lamp is the Sun. One child sits in a chair as Earth. One child holds a model Moon.

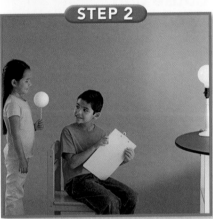
STEP 2

2. **Observe** The Moon slowly walks around Earth. Earth observes the changes in the amount of light on the Moon.

3. **Record Data** On the Moon chart, Earth records how the light and shadows on the Moon model change.

STEP 3

Think and Share

1. When did you see most of the Moon model?

2. What happened to the Moon model as it moved around the Earth model? Tell why.

Investigate More!

Work Together Switch roles so that everyone has a turn to be Earth. Compare your results. Talk about how the Moon seemed to change.

▶ **Vocabulary**

Moon

phases

▶ **Reading Skill**
Cause and
Effect

The Moon

The **Moon** is a large sphere made of rock. It is the closest large space object to Earth. As Earth rotates, the Moon seems to move across the sky at night. From Earth, you can see dark spots on the Moon. With a telescope, you can see mountains and pits, or craters, on the Moon.

Earth can be seen from the Moon.

Earth

Moon

The Moon in Motion

The Moon revolves in an orbit around Earth. It takes about one month to go around one time. The pattern repeats month after month.

▶ **CAUSE AND EFFECT** Why does the Moon seem to move across the sky?

first quarter

new

The Changing Moon

The Moon does not have its own light. It reflects the Sun's light. The Sun shines on only one side of the Moon at a time. As the Moon revolves around Earth, you may see only a part of the Moon's lighted side. The Moon looks a little different every night. The different ways the Moon looks are called **phases**. The phases repeat every four weeks.

▶ **CAUSE AND EFFECT** What causes the phases of the Moon?

full

last quarter

new

Lesson Wrap-Up

1. **Vocabulary** What is the **Moon**?

2. **Reading Skill** Why does the Moon look bright in the night sky?

3. **Use Models** How does using models help you understand real objects?

Technology Visit **www.eduplace.com/scp/** to find out more about the Moon.

Long ago, people made up stories about dark spots that they saw on the Moon. Compare one story to the facts.

The Tale of Rabbit and Coyote

by Tony Johnston
illustrated by Tomie dePaola

Now Rabbit knew of a ladder that reached into the sky. He began to climb it. Up, up, up. And he hopped all the way to the moon.

Then he hid the ladder.

Far below, he saw Coyote looking for him up in the sky. But try as he might, Coyote never found the ladder.

That is why, to this day, Coyote sits gazing at the moon.

And now and then he howls at it. For he is still *very* furious with Rabbit.

The Sun and Moon

by Patrick Moore
illustration by Paul Doherty

When you look at the moon, you can see bright and dark patches. The dark patches are called seas, but they are not real seas; there is no water in them and in fact there is no water anywhere on the moon. There are high mountains, and there are many craters, which are really holes with walls around them.

THE STARRY SKY
The **Sun** and **Moon**
Patrick Moore

Sharing Ideas

1. **Write About It** Write a story to tell why you think there are dark spots on the Moon.

2. **Talk About It** Why do you think people made up stories about what they saw in the Moon?

What Stars Can You See?

Science and You

Constellations can help you remember where some stars are in the sky.

Inquiry Skill

Compare Tell how objects or events are alike or different.

What You Need

black paper

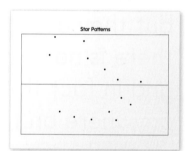

Star Patterns

star patterns

cardboard

pencil and tape

Star Pictures

Steps

1. Place one half of the black paper over the cardboard. Place a star pattern over that half of the black paper.

STEP 1

2. **Use Models** Make the star pattern on the black paper. Punch a hole for each dot.

STEP 2

3. Repeat steps 1 and 2 for the other star pattern. Tape the black paper to a window.

Think and Share

1. What pictures did you see?

2. **Compare** How are the star patterns alike and different?

STEP 3

Investigate More!

Experiment At night, go outdoors with an adult. Draw the stars that you see. Point out the brighter stars. Then look for star patterns. Share your drawings.

star

constellation

▶ **Reading Skill**

Compare and
Contrast

Stars

A **star** is a big ball of hot gases that gives off light. Stars are always in the sky. The Sun is a star. The Sun is the closest star to Earth. That is why living things on Earth are able to use the Sun's energy. The Sun's light is so bright that you cannot see any other stars during the day.

Stars are different colors. The Sun is a yellow star.

blue star

red star

At night, when our side of Earth faces away from the Sun, the sky is dark. Then you can see the other stars. They look like tiny points of light. There are so many that they are hard to count. Like the Sun, the other stars are very large. They look much smaller because they are farther away than the Sun. Some stars look brighter than others. Those stars may be bigger, hotter, or closer to Earth.

▶ **COMPARE AND CONTRAST** How are all stars alike?

yellow star

white star

Star Patterns

Some stars seem to form pictures. A **constellation** is a group of stars that forms a picture. People have named the constellations. Constellations can help you find some stars. The star Polaris is in the Little Dipper. Polaris is also called the North Star. Sailors can use the North Star to help them guide their ships.

▶ **COMPARE AND CONTRAST** What are two groups of stars that look alike?

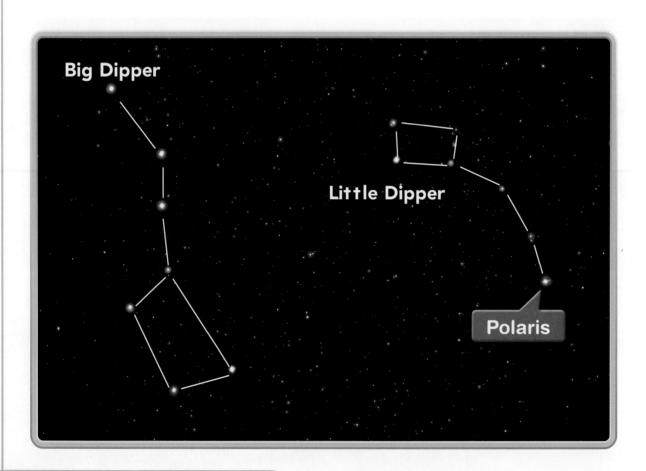

Big Dipper

Little Dipper

Polaris

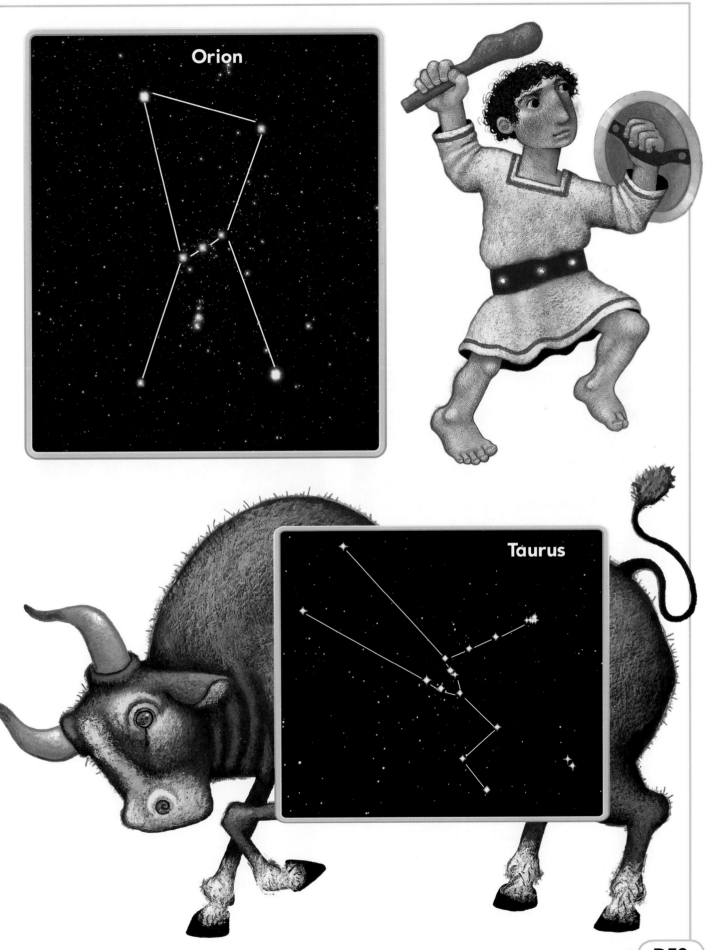

Orion

Taurus

Star Locations

Like the Moon, stars seem to move across the night sky. Earth is causing this motion. As Earth rotates, you see <u>different parts of the night sky.</u> You can see different stars in different seasons because Earth moves during the year.

Why does the Little Dipper seem to move?

Lesson Wrap-Up

❶ **Vocabulary** What is a **constellation**?

❷ **Reading Skill** How is the Sun different from other stars?

❸ **Compare** How are stars different from one another?

💻 **Technology** Visit **www.eduplace.com/scp/** to find out more about stars.

LINKS
for Home and School

Math **Use a Calendar**

This calendar shows the Moon phases for a month.

March						
Sun	Mon	Tue	Wed	Thu	Fri	Sat
					1	2
3	4	5	6	7	8	9
10	11	12	13	14	15	16
17	18	19	20	21	22	23
24	25	26	27	28	29	30
31						

1. How long does it take the Moon to go from new to full?

2. Draw a picture to show how the Moon will look on April 1.

Language Arts **Sky Flip Book**

Make a book with four cut pages like the one shown. Label the pages in the top half **Sun, Earth, Moon,** and **star**. Write about each sky object on the bottom half of the pages. Flip pages to match each word to its description.

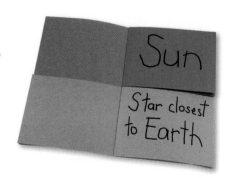

Visual Summary

Movements of Earth and the Moon cause patterns.

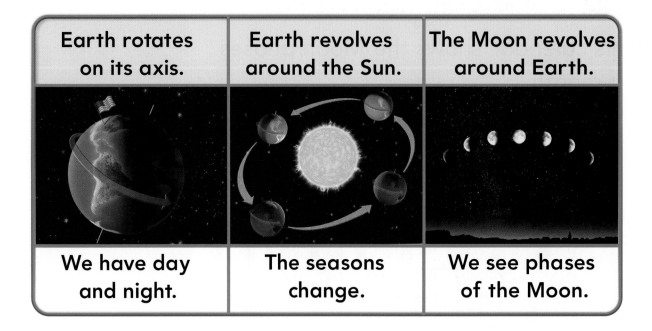

Earth rotates on its axis.	Earth revolves around the Sun.	The Moon revolves around Earth.
We have day and night.	The seasons change.	We see phases of the Moon.

Main Ideas

1. What are some objects in the solar system? (pp. D38–D39)

2. What causes night and day on Earth? (p. D42)

3. Why does the Moon appear to change? (p. D50)

4. Why do some stars look brighter than others? (p. D57)

Vocabulary

Choose the correct word from the box.

5. A big ball of hot gases that gives off light

6. A large object that moves around the Sun

7. A large sphere made of rock

8. The path that one space object travels around another

planet (p. D38)
orbit (p. D44)
Moon (p. D48)
star (p. D56)

 ## Test Practice

Choose a word to complete the sentence.

9. A _____ is a group of stars that forms a picture.

   planet constellation sphere phase

Using Science Skills

10. **Use Models** How can using models of the Sun and the Moon help you understand the Moon's phases?

11. **Critical Thinking** How does the Sun help living things?

Why doesn't it snow everywhere in winter?

Because of Earth's shape and tilt, the Sun is high in the sky in places closer to the middle of Earth every day. These places get more light and heat from the Sun all year. During winter it is usually too warm to snow in these places.

winter in California

winter in Florida

Go to **www.eduplace.com/scp/** to see why it snows in some places during winter.

Science and Math Toolbox

Using a Hand Lens H2

Using a Thermometer H3

Using a Ruler H4

Using a Calculator H5

Using a Balance H6

Making a Chart H7

Making a Tally Chart H8

Making a Bar Graph H9

Using a Hand Lens

A hand lens is a tool that makes objects look bigger. It helps you see the small parts of an object.

Look at a Coin

1 Place a coin on your desk.

STEP 1

2 Hold the hand lens above the coin. Look through the lens. Slowly move the lens away from the coin. What do you see?

3 Keep moving the lens away until the coin looks blurry.

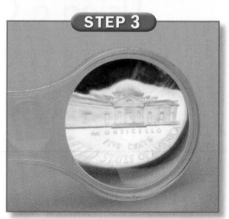
STEP 3

4 Then slowly move the lens closer. Stop when the coin does not look blurry.

STEP 4

Using a Thermometer

A thermometer is a tool used to measure temperature. Temperature tells how hot or cold something is. It is measured in degrees.

Find the Temperature of Water

1 Put water into a cup.

2 Put a thermometer into the cup.

3 Watch the colored liquid in the thermometer. What do you see?

4 Look how high the colored liquid is. What number is closest? That is the temperature of the water.

Using a Ruler

A ruler is a tool used to measure the length of objects. Rulers measure length in inches or centimeters.

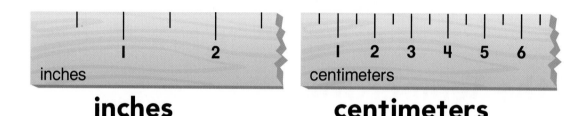

inches   **centimeters**

Measure a Crayon

1 Place the ruler on your desk.

2 Lay your crayon next to the ruler. Line up one end with the end of the ruler.

3 Look at the other end of the crayon. Which number is closest to that end?

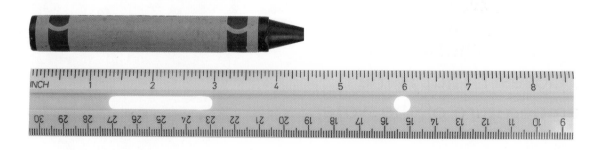

Using a Calculator

A calculator is a tool that can help you add and subtract numbers.

Subtract Numbers

1 Tim and Anna grew plants. Tim grew 5 plants. Anna grew 8 plants.

2 How many more plants did Anna grow? Use your calculator to find out.

3 Enter **8** on the calculator. Then press the **−** key. Enter **5** and press **=**.

What is your answer?

Tim's Plants

Anna's Plants

Using a Balance

A balance is a tool used to measure mass. Mass is the amount of matter in an object.

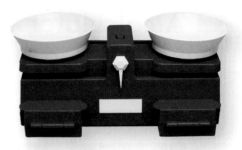

Compare the Mass of Objects

1 Check that the pointer is on the middle mark of the balance. If needed, move the slider on the back to the left or right.

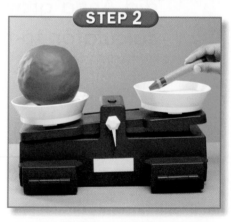

2 Place a clay ball in one pan. Place a crayon in the other pan.

3 Observe the positions of the two pans.

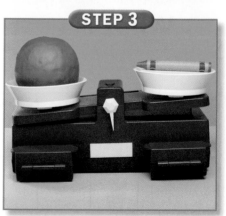

Does the clay ball or the crayon have more mass?

Making a Chart

A chart can help you sort information, or data. When you sort data it is easier to read and compare.

Make a Chart to Compare Animals

(1) Give the chart a title.

(2) Name the groups that tell about the data you collect. Label the columns with the names.

(3) Carefully fill in the data in each column.

Which animal can move in the most ways?

How Animals Move	
Animal	How it Moves
fish	swim
dog	walk, swim
duck	walk, fly, swim

Making a Tally Chart

A tally chart helps you keep track of items as you count.

Make a Tally Chart of Kinds of Pets

Jan's class made a tally chart to record the number of each kind of pet they own.

1 Every time they counted one pet, they made one tally.

2 When they got to five, they made the fifth tally a line across the other four.

3 Count the tallies to find each total.

How many of each kind of pet do the children have?

Kinds of Pets

🐱	cat	卌 ‖
🐶	dog	卌 ‖‖
🐹	hamster	‖‖

Making a Bar Graph

A bar graph can help you sort and compare data.

Make a Bar Graph of Favorite Pets

You can use the data in the tally chart on page H8 to make a bar graph.

1 Choose a title for your graph.

2 Write numbers along the side.

3 Write pet names along the bottom.

4 Start at the bottom of each column. Fill in one box for each tally.

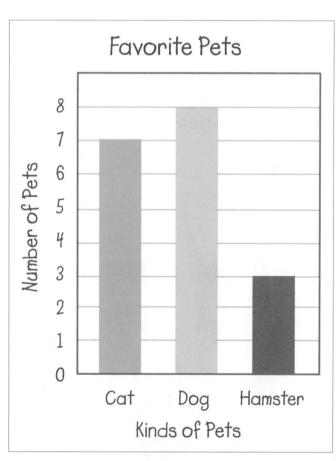

Which pet is the favorite?

Health and Fitness Handbook

When your body works well, you are healthy. Here are some ways to stay healthy.

- Know how your body works.

- Follow safety rules.

- Dance, jump, run, or swim to make your body stronger.

- Eat foods that give your body what it needs.

Your Senses.....................H12

Your senses tell you about the
world around you.

Protect Eyes and Ears.....................H14

Learn how to protect your
eyes and ears.

Staying Safe on the Road H15

Be safe when you walk or when
you ride in a car or bus.

Move Your Muscles! H16

There are many ways to
exercise your muscles.

Food Groups.....................................H17

Eat foods from different
groups.

Your Senses

Your five senses help you learn about the world. They help you stay safe.

Sight

Light enters the eye through the pupil. The iris controls how much light comes in. Other parts of the eye turn the light into messages that go to the brain.

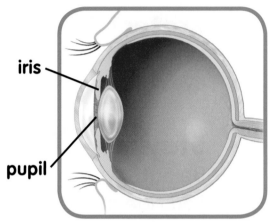

The iris is the colored part of the eye.

Hearing

The ear has three main parts. Most of your ear is inside your head. Sound makes some parts of the ear move back and forth very fast. The inner ear sends information about the sound to the brain.

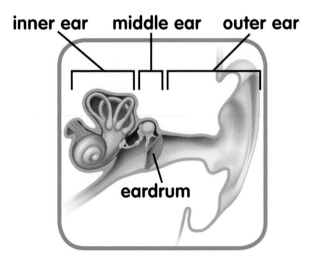

The eardrum is easily injured. Never stick anything in your ear.

Taste

Your tongue is covered with thousands of tiny bumps called taste buds. They help you taste sweet, salty, sour, and bitter things. Some parts of the tongue seem to sense some flavors more strongly. The whole tongue tastes salty foods.

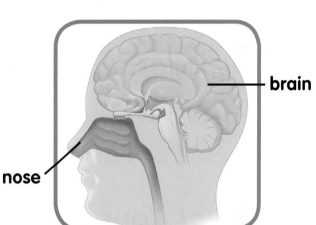

Your body makes a new set of taste buds about every two weeks.

Smell

All kinds of smells travel through the air. These smells enter your nose. Your nose sends messages to your brain about them.

Your sense of smell also helps you taste.

Touch

Touch a tree trunk, and it feels rough. A kitten feels soft. Your skin senses all this information. Then the brain decides how to respond.

Your skin is your body's largest organ.

Protect Eyes and Ears

You use your eyes and ears to see and hear. You can protect your eyes and ears.

Protect Your Eyes

- Keep sharp things away from your eyes.

- Wear sunglasses when you are outside. They protect your eyes from the Sun's rays.

An eye test can help tell if a person needs glasses.

Protect Your Ears

- Wear a helmet when you play baseball or softball.

- Loud noises can damage your ears. Keep music at a low volume.

A hearing test tells if a person has a hearing loss.

Staying Safe on the Road

How do you get to school or a playground? Here are ways to help you stay safe.

Walk Safely

- Stay on the sidewalk.

- Walk with a friend or trusted adult.

- Cross at crosswalks. Look both ways before you cross!

- Don't run between parked cars. Drivers might not see you.

Only cross when the "walk" sign is lit.

Obey crossing guards.

Car and Bus Safety

- If a bus has seat belts, wear one.

- Stay seated and talk quietly so the driver can pay attention to the road.

- Cross the street in front of a bus after all traffic stops.

Always wear your seat belt in a car.

Move Your Muscles!

All kinds of things can be exercise. Here are some ways you can make your muscles stronger.

By Yourself

- Kick a ball as far as you can. Chase it and kick it back.
- Ride your bike.
- Jump rope.
- Do jumping jacks.
- Put on music and dance.

With Others

- Play ball!
- Play tag. Run!
- Go for a hike.
- Play hopscotch.
- Play with a flying disk.

Food Groups

Food gives your body energy and what your body needs to grow. Foods in different groups help you in different ways.

Milk

Meat and Beans

Fruits

Vegetables

Grains

Pizza includes the Milk group (cheese), the Grains group (crust), and the Vegetable group (tomatoes).

What groups are in this bowl of cereal?

Picture Glossary

A

adaptation
A body part or action that helps a living thing meet its needs where it lives. (A54)

amphibian
An animal that lives part of its life in water and part of its life on land. (A44)

ask questions
Learn more about what you observe by asking questions of yourself and others.

attracts
When a magnet pulls an object toward itself. (F38)

B

bird
An animal that has feathers and wings. (A38)

C

classify
Sort objects into groups that are alike in some way.

communicate

Share what you learn with others by talking, drawing pictures, or making charts and graphs.

compare

Look for ways that objects or events are alike or different.

condenses

Changes from water vapor to drops of water. (D11)

cone

Part of a nonflowering plant where seeds form. (A20)

conserve

To use less of something to make it last longer. (C50)

constellation

A group of stars that forms a picture. (D58)

D

dissolves

Mixes completely with water. (E17)

drought

A long time with little or no rain. (B28)

E

echo

A sound that repeats when sound waves bounce off a surface. (E47)

energy

The ability to do things. Living things get energy from food. (B38)

environment

All of the living and nonliving things around a living thing. (B8)

erosion

The carrying of weathered rock and soil from place to place. (C18)

evaporates

Changes to a gas. The Sun warms water, and water evaporates. (D10)

experiment

Make a plan to collect data and then share the results with others.

Testing Magnets	
Position of the Magnets	What Happened

F

fibrous root

A root that has many thin branches. (A22)

fish
An animal that lives in water and has gills. (A46)

food web
A model that shows how different food chains are related. (B42)

flower
The plant part where fruit and seeds form. (A14)

force
A push or a pull. (F14)

food chain
The order in which energy passes from one living thing to another. (B40)

fossil
Something that remains of a living thing from long ago. (C22)

friction
A force that makes an object slow down when it rubs against another object. (F16)

fruit

The part of a flower that grows around a seed. (A14)

healthful food

A food that is good for your body. (B50)

G

gas

A state of matter that spreads out to fill a space. A gas fills the inside of a balloon. (E11)

healthful meal

A meal with foods from the different food groups. (B52)

gravity

A pull toward the center of Earth. Objects fall to the ground unless something holds them up. (C18, F11)

hibernate

To go into a deep sleep. (D27)

H

habitat

The part of an environment where a plant or an animal lives. (B10)

humus

Tiny bits of dead plants and animals in soil. (C10)

imprint
The shape of a living thing found in rock. (C22)

infer
Use what you observe and know to tell what you think.

L

larva
A wormlike thing that hatches from an egg. (A74)

lever
A bar that moves around a fixed point. (F27)

life cycle
The series of changes that a living thing goes through as it grows. (A26)

liquid
A state of matter that does not have its own shape. (E10)

litter
Trash on the ground. (C45)

living thing
Something that grows and changes. (A8)

magnify
To make objects look larger. (E26)

magnetic
An object that is attracted to a magnet. (F42)

mammal
An animal that has fur or hair and makes milk to feed its young. (A36)

magnetic field
The area around a magnet where the magnet's force acts. (F50)

mass
The amount of matter in an object. You can measure mass with a balance. (E13)

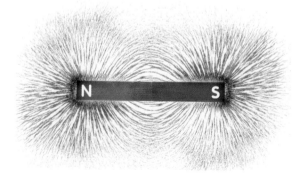

measure
Use different tools to collect data about the properties of objects.

migrate
To move to warmer places in fall. (D27)

mineral
A nonliving solid found in nature. One or more minerals form rocks. (C8)

mixture
Something made of two or more things. (E16)

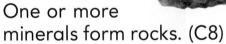

Moon
A large sphere made of rock. (D48)

motion
Moving from one place to another. (F10)

N

natural resource
Something found in nature that people need or use. (C34)

nonmagnetic
An object that is not attracted to a magnet. (F43)

offspring
The group of living things that come from the same living thing. (A64)

nutrient
A material in soil that helps a plant live and grow. Roots take in water and nutrients from the soil. (A11)

orbit
The path that one space object travels around another. (D44)

observe
Use tools and the senses to learn about the properties of an object or event.

P

phases
The different ways the moon looks. (D50)

pitch
How high or low a sound is. Cymbals have a low pitch. (E50)

planet
A large object that moves around the Sun. (D38)

pole
The place on a magnet where the force is the strongest. (F37)

pollution
Waste that harms the land, water, or air. (C45)

position
A place or location. The bird is on top of the cactus. (F8)

precipitation
Water that falls from clouds. (D12)

predict
Use what you know and patterns you observe to tell what will happen.

Testing Objects		
Object	Prediction	What Happened

properties
Color, shape, size, odor, and texture. A penny is small and round. (E8)

pulley
A wheel with a groove through which a rope or chain moves. (F28)

pupa
The stage between larva and adult when an insect changes form. (A75)

 R

ramp
A slanted tool used to move things from one level to another. (F26)

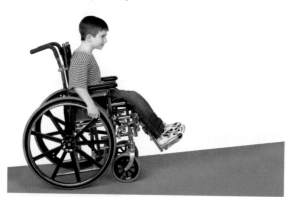

record data
Write or draw to show what you have observed.

recycle
To collect items made of materials that can be used to make new items. (C50)

repels
When a magnet pushes an object away from itself. (F39)

reproduce
To make more living things of the same kind. (A64)

reptile
An animal whose skin is covered with dry scales. (A42)

resource
Something that plants and animals use to live. (B22)

reuse
To use again and again. Old tires can be reused on a playground. (C52)

revolve
To move in a path around an object. (D44)

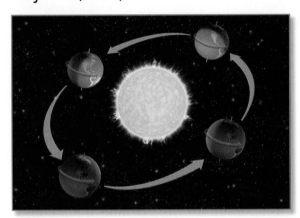

rock
A solid made of one or more minerals. (C8)

rotates
Spins around an imaginary line. (D42)

S

season
A time of year. (D16)

seed
The part from which a new plant grows. (A14)

seedling
A young plant that grows from a seed. (A26)

separate
To take apart. (E16)

shelter
A place where a living thing can be safe. (A9)

simple machine
A tool that can make it easier to move objects. (F26)

soil
The loose material that covers Earth's surface. (C10)

solar system
The Sun and the space objects that move around it. (D38)

solid
A state of matter that has its own size and shape. (E10)

sound
Energy that you hear. (E36)

sound wave
Vibrating air. (E38)

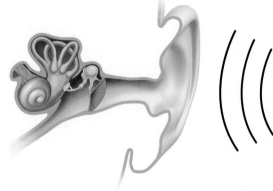

star
A big ball of hot gases that gives off light. (D56)

stream
A small river. (B14)

Sun
The brightest object in the day sky. (D36)

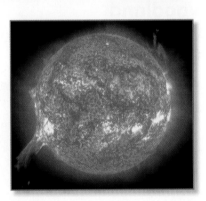

taproot
A root that has one main branch. (A22)

use data
Use what you observe and record to find patterns and make predictions.

use models
Use something like the real thing to understand how the real thing works.

use numbers
Count, measure, order, or estimate to describe and compare objects and events.

Length of Triops	
Day 1	about _____ cm
Day 2	about _____ cm
Day 3	about _____ cm
Day 4	about _____ cm
Day 5	about _____ cm

vibrates

Moves back and forth very fast. A guitar string vibrates to make a sound. (E36)

volume

1. The amount of space a liquid takes up. (E12)

2. How loud or soft a sound is. A siren is loud. (E51)

water cycle

Water moving from Earth to the air and back again. (D10)

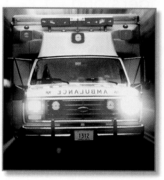

water vapor

Water as a gas. You cannot see water vapor. (D10)

weathering

The wearing away and breaking apart of rock. (C16)

woodland

A place with many trees and bushes. (B20)

work together

Work as a group to share ideas, data, and observations.

Adaptations, A33
  changing environments
    and, B30
  for desert habitats, B10
  kinds of, B11, B20
  for life on land, air, and
    water, A54–A56
  for stream habitats,
    B16–B17
  for woodland habitats,
    B20–B21
Air
  animal adaptations for,
    A56
  in environment, B8,
    B14–B16
  living things and,
    A8–A11, A30
  natural resource, C34
  pollution of, C31,
    C45–C46, C54
  in soil, C10
  sound and, E36–E39,
    E44–E45
  temperature, D18–D19,
    D37
  weather and, D8, D12
Amphibians, A44–A45,
  A49, A58, A72–A73
Animals
  amphibians, A44–A45,
    A49, A58, A72–A73
  birds, A33, A38–A39,
    A49, A58, A66,
    B16–B17, B45, B56
  body parts, A49–A51,
    B11, B32
  environment and, B8,
    B29–B30
  fish, A46–A47, A51
  food and energy,
    B38–B43, B54, C11
  groups of, A49–A51,
    A58

  habitats of, B10–B11,
    B14–B16, B20–B23
  hibernation, D5, D27
  mammals, A33,
    A36–A37, A49, A58,
    A66
  migration, D5
  needs of, A8–A9,
    A54–A56, B28, C46
  reptiles, A33, A42–A43,
    A50, A58, A66
  seasons and, D26–D27,
    D30
  of streams, B14–B16
  Sun and, D37
  of woodland habitat,
    B20–B23
Aquarium, B24–B25
Attract, F33, F38, F50,
  F54
Axis, D42, D62

Balance, E13, H6
Bats, A37, E47
Biography
  Carver, George
    Washington, C12–C13
  Merian, Maria Sibylla,
    A68–A69
Birds
  body parts, A33,
    A38–A39, A49, A53,
    A56, A58
  flamingos, B56
  herons, B16–B17
  kingfisher, B45
  life cycle of, A66
Body parts, A33,
  A49–A51, A54–A56,
  A58, B11, B32
Butterfly, A74–A75

Cactus, B10
Careers
  agriculturist, C12
  meteorologist, D9
  nature artist, A68
  scientist, A68, C22, C26
Cars, C45, F21
Carver, George
  Washington, C12–C13
Clothes, D20–D21, D28
Clouds, D11
Coal, C36
Coins, E22–E23
Color
  of animals, B20
  property of matter,
    E5, E8
Compass, F45, F56
Condense, D11
Cones, A20
Conserving, C50–C52
Constellations, D33,
  D58–D59
Cotton, C12–C13
Craters, D48, D53
Crocodiles, A43
Crops, C12–C13

Dams, C36, C44
Day, D42, D62
Daylight, D18–D19, D24,
  D31
Deer, A49, B21, D26
Desert, B10–B11, B32, B42
Dinosaurs, C24–C25, C27
Direction
  compass and, F45, F56
  and forces, F17
  sound and, E46
Dissolve, E17
Dragonfly, A76
Drought, B5, B28

Index

Ears, E38–E39, H14
Earth, C8
   changes in, C16–C19, C22–C26
   magnets and, F56
   Moon and, D38, D48–D49
   revolution of, D44–D45, D62
   rotation of, D42–D43, D60, D62
   Sun and, D36
   tilt of, D64
Echo, E47
Electricity, C36
Energy, B35
   from food, B38–B43, B48–B52, B54
   forces and, F14–F17
   plants and, C11
   sound, E33, E36–E39, E51
   from the Sun, B38, B41, D36–D37
Environment, B8–B11
   changes in, B28–B30, C44–C47, C54
   food chains in, B40–B41
   food webs in, B42
   habitats, B10–B11, B14–B17, B20–B23, B32
Erosion, C18–C19, C28
Evaporates, D10

Fall
   animals and, D26–D27
   daylight hours of, D19
   Earth's orbit and, D44–D45
   weather of, D16

Feathers, A33, A38, A49, A51, A56
Fibrous roots, A22
Fins, A51, A55, B16, B32
Fish
   body parts, A46, A51, A58, B16, B32
   habitats of, A47, B10, B15
Flamingos, B56
Flippers, A37, A55
Flood, B28
Flowers
   fruit, seeds and, A14, A20
   in spring, D24, D30
   living space and, A8
   plant part, A5, A30
Food
   healthful, B35, B50–B52
   living things and, A8, A30, B38–B43, B48–B52, B54
   plants and, A10–A11, A15, C35
   trees, B22–B23
Food chains, B35, B40–B41, B44–B45, B56
Food groups, B50–B51, H17
Food webs, B42–B43
Forces, F5, F30
   friction, F16, F20, F30
   magnetic, F33, F36–F39, F44, F50–F52
   maglev trains and, F46–F47
   motion and, F2–F3, F14–F17, F30
   safety and, F19–F21
Fossils, C5, C22–C26
Friction, F16, F20, F30
Frogs, A44–A45, A49, A72–A73
Fruit, A14, D25
Fur, A33, A36, A49, A51

Gas
   air pollution and, C45
   conserving, C50
   heat from, C37
   as resource, C41
   sound and, E44–E45, E54, E56
   state of matter, E11, E30
Gills, A44, A46, A49, A51, B16
Glacier, C18
Glass, C56
Gravity, C18–C19, F11, F19

Habitats, B5, B10–B11
   aquariums, B24–B25
   deserts, B10
   streams, B2–B3, B14–B17
   woodland, B20–B23
Hail, D11, D12
Health and Safety
   Safety in Motion, F18–F21
   Staying Safe in the Sun, D20–D21
   Unsafe Plants, A23
Healthful food, B35, B50–B52
Healthful meals, B35, B52
Hearing, E38–E39
Heat
   change of state and, E20–E21
   making, C37
   from the Sun, D10, D36
Hibernate, D5, D27
Humus, C10

Imprints, C22

Inquiry skills

ask questions, A35, A71, B7, B37, D15, E43, F6, F7, F41

be an inventor, C17, D23, E25, E49

classify, A18, A19, A62, A63, B6, B7, B46, B47, F40, F41

communicate, B13, B37, C6, C15, C21, C43, D14, D15, E25

compare, A24, A25, A40, A41, A53, A63, B27, B47, C7, C33, C43, C49, D22, D23, D54, D55, E7, E14, E15, E25, E42, E43, F12, F13, F35

experiment, A13, A25, A53, B13, B27, C33, C43, D7, D35, D55, E15, E35, F13, F23, F35, F49

infer, A12, A13, A35, A41, A53, A71, B13, B19, C15, C20, C21, C33, C43, D7, D15, D23, D35, D41, E15, E34, E35, E43, E48, E49, F23, F35

measure, A25, A71, C49, D7, D15, E6, E7, E49, F22, F23

observe, A7, A13, A19, A25, A35, A41, A63, A71, B7, C7, C15, C32, C33, D7, D40, D41, D47, E24, E25, E35, E43, E49, F7, F13, F34, F35, F41, F49

predict, A34, A35, B26, B27, D34, D35, E15, E49, F41, F48

record data, A6, A7, A19, A41, B7, B19, C7, D15, D35, D47, F7, F35

solve a problem, A7, C49

use data, A70, A71, F23

use models, A52, A53, B12, B13, B18, B19, B36, B37, C15, C43, C49, D46, D47, D55

use numbers, C48, C49, D6, D7

work together, A19, A41, A63, B47, C14, C15, C21, D41, D47, E7

Insects, A74–A76

Investigate

bird beaks, A52–A53

change the land, C14–C15

classify foods, B46–B47

classify objects, F40–F41

compare animals, A40–A41

compare fabrics, D22–D23

compare matter, E14–E15

compare samples, C6–C7

compare sounds, E42–E43

compare weather, D6–D7

feathers, A34–A35

groups, plant, A18–A19

grow a plant, A24–A25

light and heat, D34–D35

living or nonliving, B6–B7

make a food chain, B36–B37

make a pinwheel, C32–C33

make a stream, B12–B13

make imprints, C20–C21

make things move, F12–F13

making sounds, E48–E49

match animals, A62–A63

measure heat, D14–D15

measure matter, E6–E7

measure motion, F22–F23

Moon phases, D46–D47

moving water, A12–A13

needs of living things, A6–A7

observe force, F48–F49

observe motion, F6–F7

observe objects, E24–E25

observe shadows, D40–D41

observe sound, E34–E35

pollution, C42–C43

predict change, B26–B27

star pictures, D54–D55

test magnets, F34–F35

Triops changes, A70–A71

wasted water, C48–C49

woodland model, B18–B19

Iron, F42

L

Land

animal adaptations for, A54

pollution of, C31, C45–C46

temperature, D18–D19, D37

Landfill, C44

Larva, A61, A74–A75

Leaves
  grouping plants by, A21
  part of plants, A15–A17, A30
  plant life cycle and, A27
  seasons and, D24, D25, D30

Levers, F5, F27

Life cycle
  of animals, A66–A67
  of butterfly, A74–A75
  of dragonfly, A76
  of frogs, A72–A73
  of plants, A26–A28

Light
  daylight, D18–D19, D24
  shadows and, D43
  sunlight, A11, B20, B29, B38, B41, C37, D35–D37

Links for Home and School
  Art, A29, E29, F53
  Language Arts, A77, B53, C53, D61
  Math, A29, A57, A77, B31, B53, C27, C53, D29, D61, E29, E53, F29, F53
  Music, A57, E53
  Social Studies, B31, C27, D29, F29

Liquid
  changes to gas and solid, E20
  sound and, E44–E45, E54, E56
  state of matter, E10, E30

Literature
  Crawdad Creek, B2–B3
  Let's Go Rock Collecting, C2–C3
  Motion: Push and Pull, Fast and Slow, F2–F3
  "My House's Night Song," E41
  River of Life, B44–B45
  From Seed to Pumpkin, A2–A3
  The Sun and Moon, D53
  The Sun: Our Nearest Star, D2–D3
  The Tale of the Rabbit and the Coyote, D52
  What's the Matter in Mr. Whiskers' Room? E2–E3
  "Wind Song," E40

Litter, C45, C46

Living things
  adaptations of, A33, A54–A56, B10, B11, B16–B17, B20–B21, B30
  animals, A33
  environment and, B8–B11
  food and energy, B38–B43
  fossils of, C22–C26
  habitats of, B10–B11, B14–B17
  life cycle of, A5, A26–A28, A66–A67, A72–A76
  needs of, A8–A11
  offspring, A49, A61, A64–A65, A72–A73, A74, A78
  plants, A5
  reproducing, A61, A64–A65, A78
  streams and, B14–B16
  Sun and, A11, D37

Lizards, A42, B10

Maglev trains, F46–F47

Magnetic field, F33, F50, F53

Magnetic objects, F33, F42

Magnets
  compass, F45, F56
  forces and, F42–F45, F50–F52
  magnetic field, F33, F50, F53
  maglev trains, F46–F47
  objects and, F42
  poles of, F33, F37, F50
  properties of, F33, F36–F39, F54
  uses for, F44–F45

Magnify, E5, E26–E28

Mammals, A33, A36–A37, A58, A66–A67

Mass, E13

Matter, E2–E3
  changing shape and size, E18–E19, E22–E23
  changing states, E20–E21, E22–E23
  magnifying, E26–E28
  mass of, E13
  mixtures of, E16–E17
  properties of, E5, E8–E9, E30
  sound and, E44–E45
  states of, E10–E11, E30
  volume of, E12

Measuring
  lengths, A77, E29
  mass, E13
  motion, F23–F25
  volume, E12

Melting, E20–E21

Merian, Maria Sibylla, A68–A69

Meteorologists, D9

Microscope, E26–E28

Migrate, D5, D27

Minerals, C8–C9

Mixtures, E5, E16–E17

Moon
  dark spots on, D53
  Earth and, D48–D49
  phases of, D33, D50–D51, D61, D62
  and planets, D38

Index

Motion, F5
  forces and, F2–F3,
    F14–F17, F30
  measuring, F23–F25
  position and, F10–F13
Mountain habitat, B32
Mouse, A67

Natural resources, C31
  changes to environment,
    C44–C47
  conserving, C50–C52
  kinds of, C34–C37
  people and, C38–C41
  trees, B22
Night, D42, D62
Nonliving things, B8–B11,
  B14
Nonmagnetic objects,
  F43
North Star, D58
Nutrients, A10–A11,
  C12–C13

Offspring, A61, A64–A65
  of amphibians,
    A72–A73
  growth of, A78
  of insects, A74
  of mammals, A36
  of sea lions, A80
Oil
  conserving, C50
  heat from, C37
  water pollution and, C45
Orbit
  of Earth, D44–D45
  of Moon, D49
  of planets, D38–D39

Parents
  amphibians, A44,
    A72–A73
  insects, A74
  offspring and, A66–A67
  reptiles, A43, A66
  of sea lions, A80
Patterns
  of daylight, D18
  of Moon phases,
    D49–D51
  of stars, D58–D59
  of weather, D8–D9,
    D16–D17
People
  environment and, B30,
    C44–C47, C54
  food and energy for,
    B48–B52
  resources and, C38–C41
Phases of the Moon,
  D33, D50–D51
Pitch, E33, E50, E52, E53
Planets, D38–D39
Plants
  environment and,
    B8–B10, B29
  food and energy,
    B38–B43, B54
  groups of, A20–A21
  life cycle, A26–A28
  as natural resource, C35
  needs of, A8, A10–A11
  parts of, A14–A17,
    A20–A22, A30
  poisonous, A23
  as resource, C40
  seasons and, D24–D25,
    D30
  as shelter, A9
  soil and, C10–C11
  streams and, B14–B16
  Sun and, A11, D37
  water and, B28

weathering rocks,
    C16–C17
  of woodland habitat,
    B20–B23
Polaris, D58
Poles of magnets, F33,
  F37, F50
Pollution, C31, C45, C54
Position, F8–F11
Precipitation, D5, D12,
  D17
Properties
  of magnets, F33,
    F38–F39, F50, F54
  of matter, E5, E8–E9,
    E30
Pulleys, F28
Pupa, A61, A75

Quarters, E22–E23

Radar, D9
Rain, B5, B28, D9, D11,
  D12, D13
Ramps, F5, F26
Readers' Theater
  Forest Friends,
    A48–A51
  People and Resources,
    C38–C41
  Safety in Motion,
    F18–F21
Reading in Science
  Crawdad Creek, B2–B3
  *Let's Go Rock
    Collecting,* C2–C3
  *Motion: Push and Pull,
    Fast and Slow,* F2–F3

From Seed to Pumpkin, A2–A3

The Sun: Our Nearest Star, D2–D3

What's the Matter in Mr. Whiskers' Room? E2–E3

Recycle, C31, C50

Repel, F39, F50, F54

Reproduce, A61, A64–A65

Reptiles, A33, A42–A43, A50, A58, A66

Resources, C31

  changes to environment and, C44–C47

  conserving, C50–C52

  kinds of, C34–C37

  people and, C38–C41

  trees, B22

Reuse, C31, C52

Revolve, D44–D45

Rocks

  changing, C16–C17

  erosion of, C18–C19

  fossils, C5, C22–C23

  glass made from, C56

  minerals and, C5, C8–C9

  natural resource, C34

  places found, C2–C3

  as shelter, A9, B10, B15

  in soil, C10, C16

  weathering, C5, C16–C17, C28

Roots, A5, A15–A17, A22, A30

Rotation

  of crops, C12–C13

  Earth and, D33, D42–D43, D49

  stars and, D60

Scales, A33, A42, A46, A50, A51

Scientific inquiry, S6

Sea lions, A80

Seasons, D30

  animals and, D26–D27, D30

  clothes and, D28

  Earth's orbit and, D44–D45, D62

  plants and, D24–D25, D30

  stars and, D60

  weather and, D16–D17, D64

Seedlings, A5, A26, A28

Seeds, A14, A20, A26–A28, A30

Senses, B15, H12–H13

Separate, E5, E16

Shadows, D43

Shape, E5, E8, E30

Shelter, A9, B22–B23

Simple machines, F26–F28

Size, E5, E8

Sleet, D11, D12

Snakes, A43

Snow, D11, D12, D13

Soils, C5

  environment and, B8

  erosion of, C18–C19

  natural resource, C34

  nutrients in, A11

  parts of, C10–C11

Solar collector, C37

Solar system, D33, D38–D39

Solid

  changes, E18–E20

  sound and, E45, E54, E56

  state of matter, E10, E30

Sound, E33, E54

  movement of, E44–E47, E56

  pitch, E33, E50, E52, E53

  vibrations, E33, E36–E39

  volume, E33, E51–E52, E53

  wind and, E40

Sound waves, E38–E39, E44–E47, E50–E52

Space, A8, E12

Speed, F24–F25

Spring

  animals and, D26, D27

  daylight hours of, D18

  Earth's orbit and, D44–D45

  plants and, D25

  weather in, D16

Stars, D33, D56–D60

Stems, A15–A17, A21, A27, A30

Streams, B2–B3, B5, B14–B17, B32, D11

Summer

  daylight hours of, D19

  Earth's orbit and, D45

  plants and, D25

  weather in, D16

Sun

  day and night and, D42

  daylight and, D18

  Earth's orbit around, D44–D45, D62

  energy from, B38, B54, D36–D37

  food chains and, B41

  heat from, C37, D8–D10

  Moon and, D50

  plants and, A11, B20, B29, B38, B41

  reptiles and, A42

  safety in, D20–D21, D41

Index

shadows and, D43
size of, D2–D3
in solar system, D33, D38–D39
as a star, D56–D57

Taproots, A5, A22
Technology, S11
  Changing Matter to Make Coins, E22–E23
  Creating Habitats, B24–B25
  Maglev Trains, F46–F47
Temperature, D16–D17, D30
Texture, E5, E8
Thunderstorms, D9, D12
Time, D43
Tools
  balances, E7, E13, H6
  calculators, H5
  graduated cylinder, C48
  hand lenses, A35, A71, B7, C7, E25–E28, H2
  levers, F5, F27
  magnifying, E5
  measuring cup, E7, E12
  meter stick, F23
  microphone, E44
  microscope, E26–E28
  pulley, F28
  ramps, F5, F26
  rulers, A25, A71, E12, F13, H4
  simple machines, F26–F28
  to study weather, D9
  thermometers, D7, D15, D22, D35, H3
Trains, F46–F47
Trash, C44

Trees
  acorns and, A28
  cutting of, C44, C54
  fire and, B28
  needs of, A8
  parts of, A17, A21
  people and, C35
  planting, C46–C47
  pollution and, C45
  as resources, B22–B23
  as shelter, A9
  woodland habitat, B20–B23
Turtles, A42–A43, A50
Tyrannosaurus rex, C24

Vibrate, E33, E36–E39, E50–E52
Volume, E12, E33, E51–E52, E53

Water, D30
  animal adaptations for, A55
  condensing, D5, D11
  conserving, C51
  cycle of, D10–D11
  desert habitats and, B10
  in environment, B8
  erosion by, C18–C19
  fish and, A46–A47
  hot weather and, D21
  living things and, A8–A11, A30
  making electricity, C36
  Moon and, D53
  natural resource, C34, C41

  in oceans, D11
  pollution of, C31, C45, C54
  precipitation, B28, D5, D12, D17
  in soil, C10
  sound and, E44–E45
  states of, D10–D11, E20
  stream habitats, B14–B16
  temperature, D18–D19, D37
  weathering rocks, C16–C17
Water cycle, D10–D11, D31
Water vapor, D5, D10–D11, E20
Waves, C19
  sound as, E38–E39, E46–E47, E51
Weather
  changes in, D8–D9
  kinds of, D12–D13
  seasons and, D16–D17
Weathering, C5, C16–C17, C28
Whales, A37, E44
Wind, D13
  erosion by, C18–C19
  making electricity, C36
  sounds and, E40
  weathering rocks, C16–C17
Wings, A33, A37, A38, A49
Winter
  animals and, D26–D27
  daylight hours of, D18
  Earth's orbit and, D45
  plants and, D25
  weather, D16–D17, D64
Wood, C37
Woodland habitat, B5, B20–B23, B32

Credits

Permission Acknowledgements

Excerpt from The Tale of Rabbit and Coyote, by Tony Johnston, illustrated by Tomie de Paola. Text copyright © 1998 by Roger D. Johnston and Susan T. Johnston as Trustees of the Johnston Family Trust. Illustrations copyright © 1998 by Tomie de Paola. Used by permission of G.P. Putnam's Sons, a Division of Penguin Young Readers Group, A Member of Penguin Group (USA) Inc., 345 Hudson Street, New York, NY 10014, the author and Writers House LLC, acting as agent for the author. All rights reserved. Excerpt from Motion: Push and Pull, Fast and Slow, by Darlene Stille, illustrated by Sheree Boyd. Copyright © 2004 by Picture Window Books. Reprinted by permission of Picture Window Books. Excerpt from Let's Go Rock Collecting, by Roma Gans, illustrated by Holly Keller. Text copyright © 1984, 1997 by Roma Gans. Illustrations copyright © 1997 by Holly Keller. Reprinted by permission of HarperCollins Publishers. Excerpt from From Seed to Pumpkin, by Wendy Pfeffer, illustrated by James Graham Hale. Text copyright © 2004 by Wendy Pfeffer. Illustrations copyright © 2004 by James Graham Hale. Reprinted by permission of HarperCollins Publishers. Excerpt from River of Life, by Debbie S. Miller, illustrated by Jon Van Zyle. Text copyright © 2000 by Debbie S. Miller. Illustrations copyright © 2000 by Jon Van Zyle. Reprinted by permission of Clarion Books, an imprint of Houghton Mifflin Company. Excerpt from Crawdad Creek, by Scott Russell Sanders, illustrated by Robert Hynes. Text copyright © 1999 by Scott Russell Sanders. Illustrations copyright © 1999 by Robert Hynes. Reprinted by permission of National Geographic Society. Excerpt from The Starry Sky: The Sun and Moon, by Patrick Moore, illustrated by Paul Doherty. Copyright © 1994 Aladdin Books Limited. Text copyright © 1994 by Patrick Moore. Revised edition © 2000. Reprinted by permission of Aladdin Books Limited. Excerpt from The Sun: Our Nearest Star, by Franklyn M. Branley, illustrated by Edward Miller. Text copyright © 1961, 1988, 2002 by Franklyn M. Branley. Illustrations copyright © 2002 by Edward Miller III. Reprinted by permission of HarperCollins Publishers. Excerpt from My House's Night Song from My House is Singing, by Betsy R. Rosenthal. Copyright © 2004 by Betsy R. Rosenthal. Reprinted by permission of Harcourt, Inc. This material may not be reproduced in any form or by any means without the prior written permission of the publisher. *Wind Song* from *I Feel The Same Way*, by Lilian Moore. Copyright © 1967, 1995 by Lilian Moore. Reprinted by permission of Marian Reiner Literary Agency. Excerpt from What's the Matter in Mr. Whisker's Room, by Michael Elsohn Ross, illustrated by Paul Meisel. Text copyright © 2004 by Michael Elsohn Ross. Illustrations copyright © 2004 by Paul Meisel. Reproduced by permission of the publisher Candlewick Press Inc., Cambridge, MA.

Cover

(bear cub) (Spine) Daniel J. Cox/Getty Images.(Back cover bears) Tom Walker/Getty Images. (landscape) Panoramic Images/Getty Images.

Photography

Unit A Opener Martin Harvey/Wild Images. **A1** Dave Watts/Dave Watts Photography. **A4–A5** Robert W. Ginn/Photo Edit, Inc. **A5** (tc) Colin Keates/DK Images. (bc) © Dwight Kuhn. (t) Gary VestalPhotographer's Choice/Getty Images. **A6** (bl) Robert A. Ross/Color Pic, Inc. **A6–A7** (bkgd) Andrew Brown/Ecoscene/Corbis. **A9** (tr) Bob & Clara Calhoun/Bruce Coleman, Inc. (br) Jeff Foott/Bruce Coleman, Inc. **A10** (inset) Nigel Cattlin/Photo Researchers, Inc. **A10–A11** (bkgd) Michael Busselle/Taxi/Getty Images. **A12–A13** (bkgd) Kathy Atkinson/Osf/Animals Animals. **A14** (l) Philip Dowell/DK Images. (r) © Dwight Kuhn. **A16** (t) Photo 24/Brand X Pictures/Getty Images. (b) N. Et Perennou/Photo Researchers, Inc. **A17** (t) M. Loup/Peter Arnold. (b) Matthew Ward/DK Images. **A18** (b) Alan & Linda Detrick/Photo Researchers, Inc. **A18–A19** (bkgd) Adam Jones/Osf/Animals Animals. **A20** (c) Matthew Ward/DK Images. (b) Colin Keates/DK Images. **A21** (tl) William Leonard/DRK Photo. **A21** (tr), (bl), (br) Matthew Ward/Dk Images. A22 (tl), (tr) © Dwight Kuhn. **A23** (tl) Ace Stock/Alamy Images. (r) Lani Howe/Photri. (bl) Jan Stromme/Bruce Coleman, Inc. **A24–A25** (bkgd) Michael B. Gadomski/Photo Researchers, Inc. **A28** (tr) © Dwight Kuhn. **A30** (l)© E.R. Degginger/Color–Pic, Inc. (lc) M. Loup/Peter Arnold. (c) © Dwight Kuhn. (rc) Colin Keates/DK Images. (r) Matthew Ward/DK Images. **A32–A33** (bkgd) Stephen J. Krasemann/DRK Photo. **A33** (t) Brain Stablyk/Photographer's Choice/Getty Images. (tc) Skip Moody/Dembinsky Photo Associates. (bc) John Cancalosi/DRK Photo. **A33** (b) G. Staebler/Masterfile. **A34–A35** (bkgd) Leslie Newman & Andrew Flowers/Photo Researchers, Inc. **A36** Brian Stablyk/Photographer's Choice/Getty Images. A37 (cl) Alan & Sandy Carey/Photo Researchers, Inc. (br) Tom Brakefield/DRK Photo. **A38** (t) K. McGougan/Bruce Coleman, Inc. (bl) Skip Moody/Dembinsky Photo Associates. **A39** Norman Owen Tomalin/Bruce Coleman, Inc. **A40** (bl) Frans Lantig/Minden Pictures. **A40–A41** (bkgd) Maresa Pryor/Earth Scenes/Animals Animals. **A42** Rod Planck/Photo Researchers, Inc. **A43** (tr) John Cancalosi/DRK Photo. (b) S.Gatzen/EyePress/Photri. **A44** (r) Sharon Cummings/Dembinsky Photo Associates. (bl) Gay Bumgarner/Index Stock Imagery. (frog) Skip Moody/Dembinsky Photo Associates. **A45** (tr) Frans Lanting/Minden Pictures. (tl) Michael & Patricia Fogden/Minden Pictures. (cr) Scott Camazine/Photo Researchers, Inc. (b) Dwight Kuhn/Bruce Coleman, Inc. **A46** (tl) William Leonard/DRK Photo. **A46** (cl) Marilyn Kazmers/Dembinsky Photo Associates. **A46–A47** (bkgd) Avi Klapfer/Mo Yung Productions/Norbert Wu Productions. **A47** (tr) Hans Reinhard/Bruce Coleman, Inc. (cr) © E. R. Degginger/Color Pic, Inc. **A52** (bl) Medford Taylor/National Geographic Image Collection. (bkgd) David Sanger/Alamy Images. **A54** (cr) G. Staebler/Masterfile. (b) Gregory G. Dimijian/Photo Researchers, Inc. **A55** (c) P. Kobeh/Peter Arnold. (bkgd) Tobias Bernhard/Oxford Scientific Library. **A56** © E.R. Degginger/Color Pic, Inc. **A58** (tl) Brian Stablyk/Photographer's Choice/Getty Images. (tlc) Skip Moody/Dembinsky Photo Associates. (tc) Rod Planck/Photo Researchers, Inc. (tcr) Skip Moody/Dembinsky Photo Associates. (tr) Marilyn Kazmers/Dembinsky Photo Associates. (bl) Alan & Sandy Carey/Photo Researchers, Inc. (blc) K. McGougan/Bruce Coleman, Inc. (bc) S.Gatzen/EyePress/Photri. (bcr) Dwight Kuhn/Bruce Coleman, Inc. (br) © E.R. Degginger/Color Pic, Inc. **A60–A61** (bkgd) John Cancalosi/Nature Picture Library. **A61** (t) Don & Pat Valenti/DRK Photo. (tc) John Daniels/Ardea. (bc) E.R. Degginger/Color Pic, Inc. (b) Eric Lindgren/Ardea. **A62** (bl) Nigel Cattlin/Photo Researchers, Inc. **A62–A63** (bkgd) Nigel Cattlin/Photo Researchers, Inc. **A64** John Daniels/Ardea. **A65** Dick Luria/Taxi/Getty Images. **A66** (tl) David R. Frazier/Photo Researchers, Inc. (tr) Don & Pat Valenti/DRK Photo. (cl), (cr) © Dwight Kuhn. **A67** (tl) J.L. Lepore/Photo Researchers, Inc. (tr) Anthony Mercieca/Photo Researchers, Inc. (cl) © Dwight Kuhn. (cr) DK Images. **A68** (tl) The Granger Collection, New York. (b) Academy of Natural Sciences of Philadelphia/Corbis. (frame) Image Farm. **A68–A69** (b) Merian, Maria Sibylla Graff (1647–1717)/Fitzwilliam Museum, University of Cambridge, UK/The Bridgeman Art Library. **A70** (bl) Gary Meszaros/Dembinsky Photo Associates. (br) Bob Jensen/Bruce Coleman, Inc. **A70–71** (bkgd) Michael Hubrich/Dembinsky Photo Associates. **A72** (c) E.R. Degginger/Bruce Coleman, Inc. (b) © E.R. Degginger/Color Pic, Inc. (r) Gary Meszaros/Bruce Coleman, Inc. **A72–A73** (bkgd) Marion Owen/Alaska Stock.com. **A73** (l) E.R. Degginger/Bruce Coleman, Inc. (r) John Shaw/Bruce Coleman, Inc. **A74** (l), (c), (r) © E.R. Degginger/Color Pic, Inc. **A74–A75** (bkgd) Garry Black/Masterfile. **A75** (l), (r) © E.R. Degginger/Color Pic, Inc. A76 (l), (c) © Dwight Kuhn. (r) Gary Meszaros/Dembinsky Photo Associates. **A78** (tl), (tcl), (tcr), © Dwight Kuhn. (tr) DK Images. **A78** (bl), (bcl), (bcr), (br) © E.R. Degginger/Color Pic, Inc. **A80** (l), (c) Ron Sanford/Corbis. (r) Caudia Adams/Dembinsky Photo Associates. Unit B Opener Rod Williams/Nature Picture Library. **B1** Denver Bryan Photography. **B4–B5** (bkgd) Tim Davis/Corbis. **B5** (t) Jeff Hunter/Getty Images. (tc) John Shaw/Bruce Coleman, Inc. (b) Nigel Cattlin/Photo Researchers, Inc. (bc) Garry Black/Masterfile. **B6** (bl) Fritz Polking/Peter Arnold. **B6–B7** (bkgd) Terry W. Eggers/Corbis. **B8** Tom Soucek/AlaskaStock.com. **B9** (t) Bill Brooks/Masterfile. **B9** (b) Ric Ergenbright/Corbis. **B10** (t) Jeff Hunter/Photographer's Choice/Getty Images. (b) Zigmund Leszczynski/Animals Animals. **B11** (t) David Fritts/Stone/Getty Images. (cr) Wayne Lynch/DRK Photo. B12–B13 (bkgd) Darrell Gulin/DRK Photo. **B12** (bl) David T. Roberts/ Nature's Images/Photo Researchers. **B14–B15** (bkgd) John Shaw/Bruce Coleman, Inc. **B15** (tr) Stephen J. Krasemann/DRK Photo. **B16** (tl) * © Joe McDonald/Bruce Coleman, Inc. (bl) Gary Meszaros/Bruce Coleman, Inc. (r) Edward Kinsman/Photo Researchers, Inc. **B17** (tl) M.P. Kahl/Photo Researchers, Inc. (tr) Naturfoto Honal/Corbis. (cr) Jim Battles/Dembinsky Photo Associates. B18 (bl) © Gary Meszaros/Dembinsky Photo Associates. **B18–B19** (bkgd) Douglas Faulkner/Corbis. **B20** Colin Varndell/Nature Picture Library. **B21** Jim Zipp/Photo Researchers, Inc. B22 (l) Scott Camazine/Photo Researchers, Inc. (c) Jim Battles/Dembinsky Photo Associates. **B23** (tl) Wayne Bennett/Corbis. (tr) Bill Marchel/Outdoor's Finest Photography. **B24** (bl) Todd Stailey/Courtesy of Tennessee Aquarium. **B24–B25** (bkgd) Tennessee Aquarium. **B26** (bl) Gary Gray/DRK Photo. **B26–B27** (bkgd) Art Wolfe/ Imagebank/Getty Images. **B28** Nigel Cattlin/ Holt Studio International/Photo Researchers, Inc. **B29** (tr) Breck Kent/Animals Animals. (b) J. E. Swedberg/Bruce Coleman, Inc. **B30** DRK Photo. **B32** (lc) Bill Marchel/Outdoor's Finest Photography. (cr) Zigmund Leszczynski/Animals Animals. (l) Edward Kinsman/Photo Researchers, Inc. (r) David Fritts/ Stone/Getty Images. **B34–B35** (bkgd) Kevin Dodge/Masterfile. **B35** (t) Jean–Michael Cornet/Stock Image/Pixland/Alamy Images. (b) Richard Hutchings/Photo Edit, Inc. (bc) C Squared Studios/Photodisc/Getty Images. **B36** (bl) Laura Riley/Bruce Coleman, Inc. **B36–B37** (bkgd) Johnny Johnson/DRK Photo.**B38** Harry Rogers/Photo Researchers, Inc. **B39** (l) © Bill Beatty/Wild+Natural. (r) Anup Shah/ Taxi/Getty Images. **B41** (t) Peter Finger/Corbis. (c) Lynn Stone/Index Stock Imagery/PictureQuest. (b) Superstock/PictureQuest. **B46** (br) Brian Sytnyk/Masterfile. **B46–B47** (bkgd) Cosmo Condina/Getty Images. **B48** (c) J. C. Carton/Bruce Coleman, Inc. (bl) VCL/Taxi/Getty Images. **B48–B49** (b) David P. Hall/Masterfile. **B49** (r) Judd Pilloss of FoodPix. **B50** Ross Whitaker/Imagebank/Getty Images. **B52** (t) Richard Hutchings/Photo Edit, Inc. (blc) Burke/Triolo/Brand X/PictureQuest. (bl), (bc) Photodisc/Getty Images. (br) Comstock Images. **B54** (tr) Lynn Stone/Index Stock Imagery/PictureQuest. (bl) Laura Riley/Bruce Coleman, Inc. (br) Brian Sytnyk/Masterfile. **B56** (l) Mike Kelly/The Image Bank/Getty Images. (c) John Downer/Taxi/Getty Images. (r) Frank Krahmer/The Image Bank/Getty Images. Unit C Opener (bkgd) Index Stock Imagery/Alamy Images. **C1** Gary Ladd Photography. **C4–C5** (bkgd) Arthur M. Greene/Bruce Coleman, Inc. **C5** (t) Tony Freeman/Photo Edit, Inc. (c) David Young–Wolff/Photo Edit, Inc. (bc) Rod Planck/Photo Researchers, Inc. (b) Tom Bean/DRK Photo. **C6–C7** (bkgd) Jeff Foott/Bruce Coleman, Inc. **C8–C9** (bkgd) Dennis MacDonald/Photo Edit Inc. **C9** (tl), (tc) Tony Freeman/Photo Edit Inc. (tr) © Panographics Science Stock. (bl) Roger Wood/Corbis. (bc) Phil Degginger/Color Pic, Inc. (br) Owen Franken/Corbis. **C11** (tl) John William Banagan/ The Image Bank/Getty Images. (tc) E.R. Degginger/Color Pic, Inc. (tr) David Young–Wolff/Photo Edit Inc. **C12** (tl) Hulton Archive/ Stringer/Getty Images. (b) Bettmann/Corbis. **C12–C13** (bkgd) Brian K. Miller/Animals Animals/Earth Scenes. **C13** (t) YardDoctor.com/Briggs and Stratton. (lc) F. Damm/Masterfile. (rc) Jane Grushow/Grant Heilman Photography. **C14–C15** (bkgd) © Susan E. Degginger/Color Pic, Inc. **C16** J. David Andrews/Masterfile. **C17** (tl) E.R. Degginger/Color–Pic, Inc. (tr) Rod Planck/Photo Researchers, Inc. (b) Tom Bean/DRK Photo. **C18** Stephen J. Krasemann/DRK photo. **C19** (t) Brian Miller/Bruce Coleman, Inc. (cr) Thomas Dressler/DRK Photo. **C20** (bl) Francois Gohier/Photo Researchers, Inc. **C20–C21** (bkgd) Kazimieras Mizgiris/AFIAP/Mizgiris Amber Museum. **C23** (tr) Alvis Upitis/Superstock. (cr) William P. Leonard/DRK Photo. (br) Mindy McNaugher/Stock Photo Archives/Carnegie Museum of Natural History. **C24–C25** (c) DK Images. **C25** (t) Bob Jensen/Bruce Coleman, Inc. (br) Frank Staub/Index Stock Imagery. **C26** (tr) Francois Gohier/Photo Researchers, Inc. (cr) Tom bean/DRK Photo. (br) T. A. WieWandt/DRK Photo. **C27** (br) Bill Aaron/Photo Edit, Inc. **C28** (tr) J. David Andrews/Masterfile. (tl) Rod Planck/Photo Researchers, Inc. (bl) Thomas Dressler/DRK Photo. (br) Brian Miller/Bruce Coleman, Inc. **C30–C31** (bkgd) ©Dwight Kuhn. **C31** (t) Buddy Mays/Corbis. (tc) E.R. Degginger/Color Pic, Inc. (bc) Arnold John Kaplan/Photri. (b) Corbis. **C32** (bl) Jock Montgomery/Bruce Coleman, Inc. **C32–C33** (bkgd) Jonathan Nourok/Photo Edit Inc. **C34** David Young–Wolff/Photo Edit, Inc. **C35** (tl) Susan Van Etten/Photo Edit, Inc. (tr) Ingram Publishing/Index Stock/Alamy Images. (c) Buddy Mays/Corbis. (br) Michael D. L. Jordan/Dembinsky Photo Associates. (bl) C Squared Studios/Getty Images. **C36** (tl) Michael E. Lubiarz/Dembinsky Photo Associates. **C36–C37** (bkgd) Jeremy Woodhouse/DRK Photo. **C37** (tr) Andrew Rakoczy/Bruce Coleman, Inc. (cr) ©Phil Degginger/Color Pic, Inc. **C42** (bl) Joe Macdonald/Bruce Coleman, Inc. **C42–C43** (bkgd) E.R. Degginger/Bruce Coleman, Inc. **C44** Paul Conklin/Photo Edit, Inc. **C45** (t) Jonathan Nourok/Photo Edit, Inc. (br) © E.R. Degginger/Color Pic, Inc. **C46** Jim West/The Image Works. **C47** (l) Steven C Kaufman/DRK Photo. **C47** (r) Darrell Gulin/DRK Photo. **C50** Arnold John Kaplan/Photri. **C51** (tl) Superstock. (tr) Charles Orrico/Superstock. (br) Myrleen Ferguson Cate/Photo Edit, Inc. **C52** Richard Hutchings/Photo Edit, Inc. **C54** (tl) © E.R. Degginger/Color Pic, Inc. (tr) Jim West/The Image Works. (cl) Jonathan Nourok/Photo Edit, Inc. (cr) Steven C Kaufman/DRK Photo. (bl) Emmanuel Faure/SuperStock. (br) Darrell Gulin/DRK Photo. **C56** (l), (c) Courtesy of Spectrum Glass. (r) Kevin Fleming/Corbis. Unit D Opener NTPL/Ian Shaw/The Image Works. **D1** Image Source/PictureQuest. **D4–D5** (bkgd) Warren Faidley/Weather Stock. **D5** (t) Andy Crawford/DKImages. (tc) Gary Meszaros/Photo Researchers, Inc. (bc) Jeff Foott/PictureQuest. (b) Jacana/Photo Researchers, Inc. **D6** (bl) Frank LaBua/Photri. **D6–D7** (bkgd) Corbis. **D8–D9** (bkgd) Don Nauman. **D9** (bc) Tom Warner/Noaa. **D10–D11** (bkgd) Jim Steinberg/Photo Researchers, Inc. **D12** (cl) Gary Meszaros/Photo Researchers, Inc. (b) Scott Smith/Index Stock Imagery. **D13** (t) Jim Mone/AP Wide World Photo. **D14** (bl) Kike Calvo/Bruce Coleman, Inc. **D14–D15** (bkgd) Carol Mallory/Dembinsky Photo Associates. **D15** (inset) Alison Barnes Martin/Masterfile. **D16** (bl) Dawn Charging/Bismark – Mandan CVB. **D17** (cr) Kindra Clineff/Index Stock Imagery. (b) Ralph Krubner/Mira. **D22** (bl) Sid & Shirley Rucker/DRK Photo. **D22–D23** (bkgd) Maslowski Photo/Photo Researchers, Inc. **D24** (t) Bill Beatty. (b)Fred Habegger/Grant Heilman Photography. **D25** (tl) Harry Rogers/Photo Researchers, Inc. (tc) Thase Daniel/Bruce Coleman Inc. (tr) Edward L. Snow/Bruce Coleman Inc. (bl) Fred Habegger/Grant Heilman Photography. (bc) Geoff Bryant/Photo Researchers, Inc. (br) Fred Habegger/Grant Heilman Photography. **D26** (bl) Photri. (b) Daniel J Cox/Natural Selection Stock Photography. **D27** (tr) Jeff Foott/PictureQuest. (tcr) S. Charles Brown; Frank Lane Picture Agency/Corbis. (cr) Bill Beatty/Animals Animals. (b) Fred Bruemmer/DRK Photo. **D30** (tr) Thase Daniel/Bruce Coleman, Inc. (tl) Edward L. Snow/Bruce Coleman Inc. (tcl) Bill Beatty. (tcr) Harry Rogers/Photo Researchers, Inc. (bcl) S. Charles Brown; Frank Lane Picture Agency/Corbis. (bcr) Bill Beatty/Animals Animals. (bl) Jeff Foott/PictureQuest. (br) Fred Bruemmer/DRK Photo. **D32–D33** (bkgd) John Henry Williams/Bruce Coleman, Inc. **D33** (bc) John Sanford/Photo Researchers, Inc. (b) Roger Ressmeyer/Corbis. **D34** (bl) Nasa/Photri. **D34–D35** (bkgd) Nasa/Photri. **D36** Nasa/Science Photo Library/Photo Researchers, Inc. **D37** (t) © Eric O'Connell/Iconica/Getty Images. **D40** (bl) World Perspectives/Photographer's Choic/Getty Images. **D40–D41** (bkgd) Bill Aron/Photo Edit, Inc. **D46** (bl) World Perspectives/Stone/Getty Images. **D46–D47** Steven Satushek/Botanica/Getty Images. **D48** World Perspectives/Stone/Getty Images. **D50–D51** (bkgd) John Sanford/Photo Researchers, Inc. **D54–D55** (bkgd) Bill Frymire/Masterfile. **D56** (cl) Eckhard Slawick/Photo Researchers, Inc. **D56–D57** (bkgd) Michael Simpson/ Taxi/Getty Images. (cr) Photri. **D57** (cl) Susan McCartney/Photo Researchers, Inc. (br) Photri. **D58** Roger Ressmeyer/Corbis. **D59** (tl) Roger Ressmeyer/Corbis. (br) John Sanford & David Parker/ Science Photo Library/Photo Researchers, Inc. D64 (l) Owaki–Kulla/Corbis. (r) Tony Arruza/Corbis. Unit E Opener Thinkstock/PictureQuest. **E1** Thinkstock/PictureQuest. **E4–E5** (bkgd) Everett Kennedy Brown, Staff/ European Press Photo Agency, EP/AP Wide World Photo. **E5** (b) Iverson/Folio Inc. **E6** (bl) Gusto/Photo Researchers, Inc. **E6–E7** (bkgd) Thom Lang/Corbis. **E13** (br) G K & Vikki Hart/Getty Images. **E23** (c) Image Courtesy of the United States. **E24** (bl) Skip Moody/Dembinsky Photo Associates, Inc. **E24–E25** (bkgd) George D. Lepp/Corbis. **E26** Ralph A. Clevenger/Corbis. **E27** (t) Jose Luis Pelaez, Inc./Corbis. (lc) Jim Zuckerman/Corbis. (rc) Iverson/Folio Inc. (b) Greg Wahl–Stephens/AP Wide World Photo. **E28** (tl) Mark A. Schneider/Dembinsky Photo Associates. (tr) Darrell Gulin/Corbis. (tc) Skip Moody/Dembinsky Photo Associates. (bc), (bl) Iverson/Folio Inc. (br) Clouds Hill Imaging Ltd./Corbis. **E32–E33** (bkgd) Daniel Bosler/Stone/Getty Images. **E33** (b) Gabe Palmer/Corbis. (bc) Premium Stock/Corbis. **E34–E35** (bkgd) Image100/Alamy Images. **E39** Michael Newman/Photo Edit, Inc. **E42** (bl) A. Ramey/Photo Edit, Inc. **E42–E43** David Madison/Photodisc/Getty Images. **E44** Flip Nicklin/Minden Pictures. **E45** Michael Newman/Photo Edit, Inc. **E46** Michael Newman/PhotoEdit, Inc. **E48–E49** Howie Garber/Animals Animals. **E50** (tl), (br) C. Squared Studios/Photodisc/Getty Images. (tr), (bl) PhotoDisc/Getty Images. (cl) Premium Stock/Corbis. (cr) Cyril Laubscher/DK Images. **E51** (tl) Gabe Palmer/Corbis. **E53** (t) C Squared Studios/Getty Images. (l) Photodisc/Getty Images. (r) Steve Cole/Getty Images. (b) David Murray/DK Images. Unit F Opener Tek Image/Photo Researchers Inc. **F1** (bkgd) Steve Taylor/Stone/Getty Images. **F4–F5** (bkgd) Joe McBride/Photgrapher's Choice/Getty Images. **F5** (t) Tony Freeman/Photo Edit, Inc. (b) © Phil Degginger/Color–Pic, Inc. **F6–F7** (bkgd) Thinkstock/Getty Images. **F10** (cl) Tony Freeman/Photo Edit, Inc. (br) Picture Plain/Photo Library.com. **F11** (tl) John Fox/Alamy Images. (br) RubberBall Productions/Getty Images. **F12–F13** (bkgd) Rolf Bruderer/Corbis. **F15** (br) Barry Runk/Grant Heilman Photography. **F16** (tl) Philip Gatward/DK Images. **F17** Rubberball Productions/Getty Images. **F24–F25** David Madison/Stone/Getty Images. **F25** (tr) Alan Thornton/Stone/Getty Images. **F26** (cr) Bob Daemmrich/Corbis Sygma. **F27** (tr) © E.R. Degginger/Color–Pic Inc. (cr) © Phil Degginger/Color–Pic Inc. F28 (l) Kimberly Robbins/Photo Edit, Inc. **F30** (tc) Barry Runk/Grant Heilman Photography. (tr) Philip Gatward/DK Images. (bl) John Fox/Alamy Images. (bc) Picture Plain/Photo Library. com. (br) Tony Freeman/Photo Edit, Inc. **F33** (tc) Michael Newman/Photo Edit, Inc. **F40** (bl) Michael Newman/Photo Edit, Inc. **F40–F41** (bkgd) Image Source Limited/Index Stock Imagery. **F44** (cr)Tom Pantages. (bl) © E.R. Degginger/Color Pic, Inc. **F45** (tr) © Phil Degginger/Color Pic, Inc. **F46–47** (bkgd) LIU Jin/AFP/Getty Images. **F48** (bl) Tim Pannell/Corbis. **F56** (r) David Young–Wolf/Photoedit, Inc.

Assignment

A6, A7 © HMCo./Ken Karp Photography. **A12, A13, A18** © HMCo./Richard Hutchings Photography. **A19** © HMCo./Lawrence Migdale Photography. **A24** (tc),(bc) © HMCo./Ken Karp Photography. **A24** (t),(br) © HMCo./Richard Hutchings Photography. **A25** (t) © HMCo./Ken Karp Photography. **A34, A35** © HMCo./Richard Hutchings Photography. **A40, A41, A48, A49, A52, A53, A62, A63** © HMCo./Ken Karp Photography. **A70** (bc) © HMCo./Richard Hutchings Photography **A70** (t),(tc),(b) **A71** © HMCo./Ken Karp Photography. **B6** (t) © HMCo./Richard Hutchings Photography. **B7** © HMCo./Lawrence Migdale Photography. **B12, B13, B18, B26, B27, B36, B37, B46, B47** © HMCo./Richard Hutchings Photography. **C6, C7, C14, C15, C20, C21, C32, C33** © HMCo./Richard Hutchings Photography. **C38** © HMCo./Ken Karp Photography. **C42, C43, C48, C49** © HMCo./Richard Hutchings Photography. **D6, D7** © HMCo./Richard Hutchings Photography. **D14** (c) © HMCo./Ken Karp Photography. **D14** (t) © HMCo./Richard Hutchings Photography. **D15,D20** © HMCo./Ken Karp Photography. **D22, D23, D28, D34, D35, D40, D41** © HMCo./Richard Hutchings Photography. **D43** © HMCo./Bud Endress Photography. **D46, D47, D54** (t), (bc), (b) © HMCo./Coppola Studios Inc. **D54** (bl) © HMCo./Ken Karp Photography. **D55** © HMCo./Richard Hutchings Photography. **E5** © HMCo./Ken Karp Photography. **E6** (t), (tc), (bc) © HMCo./Richard Hutchings Photography. **E6** (b) © HMCo./Ken Karp Photography. **E7** © HMCo./Richard Hutchings Photography. **E10–E11** © HMCo./Bud Endress Photography. **E12** © HMCo./Richard Hutchings Photography. **E13** © HMCo./Ken Karp Photography. **E14, E15** © HMCo./Richard Hutchings Photography. **E16, E17, E18, E19, E20, E21** © HMCo./Ken Karp Photography. **E24, E25, E33** (t) © HMCo./Richard Hutchings Photography. **E33** (tc), **E34** (bl) © HMCo./Ken Karp Photography. **E34** (t), (tc), (bc), (b), **E35, E36–E37, E38, E42, E43, E48, E49, E51, E52** © HMCo./Richard Hutchings Photography. **F5** (tc) © HMCo./Lawrence Migdale Photography. **F5** (bc), **F6** (b) © HMCo./Ken Karp Photography. **F6** (tr), **F7** © HMCo./Richard Hutchings Photography. **F8–F9** © HMCo./Ken Karp Photography. **F12, F13** HMCo./Richard Hutchings Photography. **F14** © HMCo./Ken Karp Photography. **F15, F16** © HMCo./Lawrence Migdale Photography. **F18, F20** © HMCo./Ken Karp Photography. **F22** © HMCo./Richard Hutchings Photography. **F22** (bkgd) © HMCo./Ken Karp Photography. **F23** © HMCo./Richard Hutchings Photography. **F26** © HMCo./Ken Karp Photography. **F30** © HMCo./Ken Karp Photography. **F33** (t) © HMCo./Richard Hutchings Photography. **F33** (bc) © HMCo./Ken Karp Photography. **F34, F35, F36, F37** © HMCo./Richard Hutchings Photography. **F38** © HMCo./Ken Karp Photography. **F39, F40, F41,** © HMCo./Richard Hutchings Photography. **F42, F43, F48** (bl) © HMCo./Ken Karp Photography. **F48** (t), **F49** © HMCo./Richard Hutchings Photography. **F51, F52** © HMCo./Ken Karp Photography.

Illustration

A5 Wendy Smith. **A8** Jeff Wack. **A15, A26–A27** Wendy Smith. **A28** Lori Anzalone. **A48–A51** Liz Conrad. **B16–B17** Luigi Galante. **B20–B21** Michael Maydak. **B22–B23** Patrick Gnan. **B35** © Lelend Klanderman. **B40–B43** © Leland Klanderman. **B51** Argosy Publishing. **B54** © Leland Klanderman. **C10** Richard Orr. **C22–C23** Michigan Science Art. **C26** Michael Maydak. **C38–C41** Theresa Smythe. **C48** Tim Johnson. **C50–C51** Digital Dimensions. **D16–D17** Robert Schuster. **D16–17** (map) Annette Cable. **D18–D19** Kristin Barr. **D21** Mark & Rosemary Jarman. **D20–D21** (bkgd) JoAnn Adinolfi. **D33** (t) Bob Kayganich. **D33** (tc) Patrick Gnan. **D38–D39** Bob Kayganich. **D42** Patrick Gnan. **D44** Argosy. **D49** Patrick Gnan. **D59** Matthew Trueman. **D60** Argosy Publishing. **E14–E15, E18–E19** Tim Johnson. **E22–E23** Robert Schuster. **E30** Terri Chicko **E33, E38** Sharon and Joel Harris. **E40** Laura Ovresat. **E41** Shane McGowan. **E47** Patrick Gnan. **E54** Terri Chicko. **E56** David Klug. **F18–F21** John Berg. **F28** George Baquero. **F47, F56** Patrick Gnan.

Nature of Science

PHOTOGRAPHY: (solar disc) © Brand X Pictures/The Stocktrek Corp/Alamy Images. **S1** © Jose Luis Pelaez, Inc./CORBIS. **S2-3** JSC/NASA. **S4-5** © Ernest Manewal/Superstock. **S5** (br) © HMCo./Ed Imaging. **S6-7** Stephen Dalton/NHPA. **S7** (r) © HMCo./Ed Imaging. **S8-9** © HMCo./Joel Benjamin Photography. **S10-1** Lloyd C. French/JPL/NASA. **S11** (r) © Reuters/CORBIS. **S12-3** (bkgd) © David Martyn Hughes/Alamy Images. **S12-3** (l) (m) (r) © HMCo./Bruton Stroube. **S14-15** © Craig Steven Thrasher/Alamy Images. **S16** © HMCo./Richard Hutchings Photography.

Health and Fitness Handbook

PHOTOGRAPHY: **H10** © Ariel Skelley/Corbis. **H13** George Shelley/Masterfile. **H14** (t) Picturequest. (b) Photodisc/Getty Images. **H15** (t) Brad Rickerby/Getty Images. (m) Rubberball/Getty Images. (b) Photodisc/Getty Images. **H16** (t) Dex Image/Getty Images. (b) Ariel Skelley/Corbis. ILLUSTRATION: **H18–H19** William Melvin. **H23** Linda Lee.

Science and Math Toolbox

H7 (t) John Giustina/Getty Images. (m) Georgette Douwma/Getty Images. (b) Giel/Getty Images. **H8** Photodisc/Getty Images.

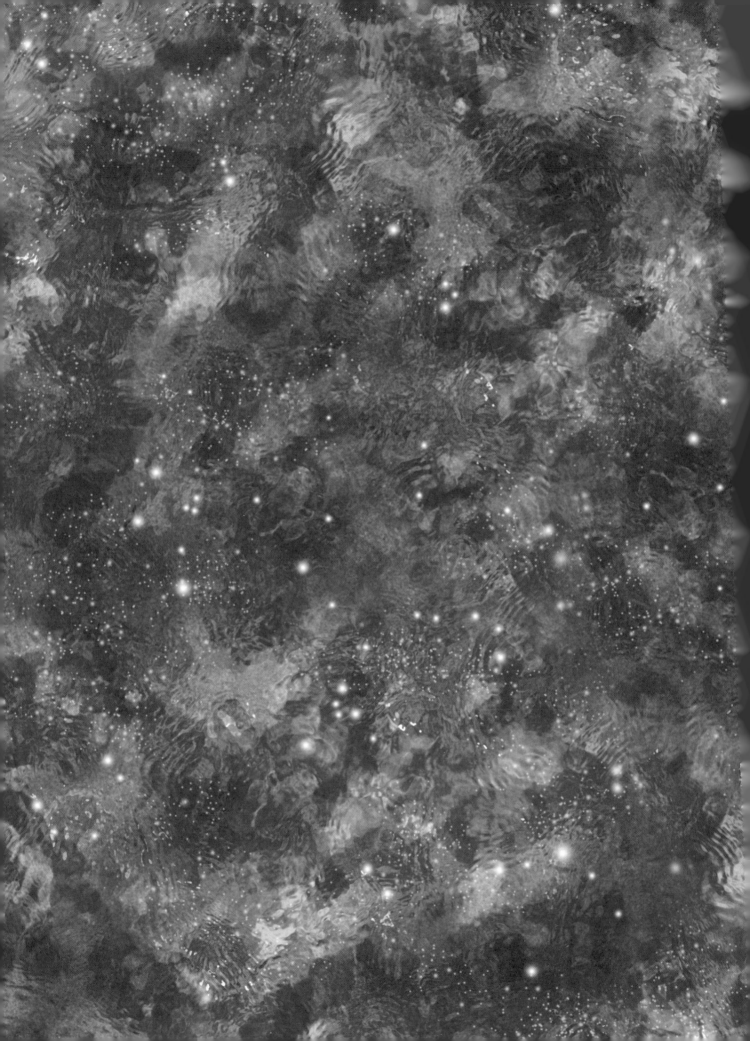